THE
FITTED
GARDEN

THE
FITTED
GARDEN
WALL TO WALL GARDEN DESIGN

DEREK MANSFIELD

Ward Lock Limited · London

First published in Great Britain in 1987
by Ward Lock Limited, 8 Clifford Street
London W1X 1RB, an Egmont Company

House editor Denis Ingram
Designed by Niki fforde
Text set in Garamond
by Latimer Trend & Company Ltd, Plymouth

Printed and bound in Italy by
Canale SpA

British Library Cataloguing in Publication Data
Mansfield, Derek
    The fitted garden: wall-to-wall garden design
    1. Gardens—Design
    I. Title
    712'.6   SB472

ISBN 0–7063–6407–4

· C O N T E N T S ·

PREFACE   6
ACKNOWLEDGEMENTS   7
 1   INTRODUCTION   9
 2   THE TRADITIONAL ENGLISH GARDEN   12
 3   COURTYARDS   23
 4   ORIENTAL GARDENS   35
 5   SPLIT LEVELS   48
 6   WATER GARDENS   61
 7   ROCK GARDENS   73
 8   A CHILDREN'S GARDEN   83
 9   DESIGNS FOR THE DISABLED   89
10   CO-ORDINATED COLOUR SCHEMES   96
11   PITFALLS, PRICES AND PLANNING   107
12   MATERIALS AND FUTURE TRENDS   115
INDEX   126

· P R E F A C E ·

In writing this book I have attempted to re-introduce an old concept to the art of landscape design. The concept is very simple. One selects a basic theme and the theme is then reflected throughout the detailed planning of the garden. In truth one cannot claim this idea as being original as total concept gardens were created by the Romans a couple of thousand years ago.

However, there is very little evidence that the contemporary garden designer ever tries to progress much beyond a pretty hotch potch. Until the landscaping fraternity learns to take a leaf from the 'Designer Range' ideas they will remain the poor relations of the design business and many gardens will remain rectangular lawns surrounded by weed-filled flower beds.

When considering ideas for interior decor one might decide the drawing room is to be Regency in style and the dining room high tech. The basic colour scheme is laid down and the wallcoverings and carpets are co-ordinated and fitted. The furniture and furnishings are then selected to complete the overall theme. And the task is simplified by famous designers lending their names to co-ordinated ranges of products.

In this book you will find examples of 'total themes' which I hope will help stimulate your own ideas and will allow you to conceive and create a garden in the same way that interior design is considered and organized. Think through the overall concept first and decide on the plants later. This is precisely the process that one decides on the theme of a room with the selection of the ornaments left to enhance the overall effect.

Taking up this concept will, I trust, both simplify the initial task of garden design and enable you to create a truly individual and stimulating garden environment. And I know you will derive a great deal of pleasure and satisfaction from your efforts. Moreover, you will be one of the few individuals who has actually planned a garden to fit.

Several people have assisted in the creation of this book and none more so than my wonderful wife Gabrielle whose indefatigable support helped me finish the book. Many thanks are also due to to the construction personnel who translated ideas into reality, notably Richard Bartlett and David Alesworth and to designers Jane Lovett-Turner, Anne Shaw and Claire Halstead.

D. S. M.

·ACKNOWLEDGEMENTS·

The publishers are grateful to the following for granting permission to reproduce the following photographs: Japanese Tourist office (pp 36 & 37); Taylor Woodrow Homes Ltd (p 41); J. Delraux (p 116); Marshalls Mono Ltd (pp 118 & 119); and Blockley plc (p 120). All the remaining photographs were taken by Bob Challinor.

The publishers are especially grateful to the following for allowing us to photograph their gardens: Peter Sutherland and Alan Harris (p 12); Sylvia Lansberg of the Tudor House Museum, Southampton; Mr & Mrs R Schwab (p 23); W. Morris Esq (p 30); Mr & Mrs Conroy (pp 43 & 81 (lower)); Mr & Mrs R Raywood (p 50); R Penny Esq (pp 53 & 81 (top)); Mr & Mrs R Finch (p 59); Mrs J Milne (pp 66, 68, 69 & 71); Patricia Wood (pp 96 & 99); Paul Lidster and Tony Foskelt (p 100); and Haddonstone Ltd (pp 61, 62 & 63).

All line drawings were drawn by Nils Solberg.

DEDICATION

For my father; the original inspiration.
For my mother; her quiet determination.
And for Norman; 'in quiet gratitude'.
But mostly for Gabrielle; her belief and understanding.

1 · INTRODUCTION ·

My main concern in writing this book is to highlight an area that I feel has been disregarded for far too long among our nation of gardeners. My concern, specifically, is the structural design of the garden rather than the plants to go into it. For example, if you were designing a kitchen you would be concerned firstly with the functions that the kitchen must perform and from this analysis you would determine what machinery is required and where it should be positioned. Having arrived at your conclusions you would select and assemble the various units within the theme you have now determined. Only at this point would you actually start looking for the pretty accoutrements of crockery, matching teapots and wall clocks.

This book, then, is designed to help you design your own garden after first considering what you wish to do in the garden (and with whom!). By using the themes and ideas contained herein it will also help if you wish to give a very tight brief to a landscape contractor. So many people have found it is very difficult to communicate their creative ideas to others and thus have had to compromise with neither party feeling particularly satisfied. A very good example of the difficulties that can occur is with the creation of rockeries. You may have in mind towering granite bluffs covered in lichen that you have seen in a National Trust forest; but if your garden is only forty metres square and in a terrace with no access, you may not be prepared to pay £1500 for the necessary crane to lift the rocks over your house. If you first consider these difficulties, and explain your requirements to your landscaper then between you, you can create a corner of your garden in perfect miniature. If this rockery is of major importance to you, but because of the garden size it must be in miniature, then it may well be that the inspiration of your whole garden should be from the masters of miniaturization. Give your garden a Japanese theme.

I have always found that when I am designing for clients it is simplest in the early stages of planning to show them a variety of garden themes in order to determine the type of garden they feel comfortable with. My personal preference is for the Avant Garde and Oriental, for both these styles require considerable design detail. On the other hand, stark expanses of black basalt with glass prisms containing holograms of plants might not suit the owners of a thatched cottage in Sussex.

The chapters in the book are divided into themes so that you can get a feeling of the type of garden that suits you, but before becoming committed to a Tudor garden because you live in a mock Tudor house let us first examine the functions of your garden.

When I ask people what do they do in their gardens and with whom they invariably answer with a shy smile and say: 'Relax with my husband/wife.' But by answering all the following questions you will discover that you either do or can use your garden for a wide range of activities. In the same way that a dining room is designed to eat in but not to take a bath in, then your garden can be designed as an open space with areas for separate activities drawn together within an overall theme.

A few words here on colour co-ordination. It astonishes me that in this age of design sophistication that the average garden centre still has not considered displaying and selling plants in co-ordinated size and 'colour-ways'. It is not my intention to cover the topic in this book but I have included examples of colour co-ordination in the garden by using stained or painted wood. For those of you who are designing gardens for new homes it is unlikely that your garden will mature for three to five years. By planning the hard surfaces in your garden to co-ordinate with both the textures and colours of those inside and outside your home you can create a co-ordinated and colourful garden from the very beginning.

Consider all the questions posed below and as you read the other chapters many of the answers will be found from the examples given. When you have found the answers to suit your particular needs decide on the overall theme and sketch your ideas into a scaled plan of your garden.

It is of paramount importance to emphasize the overall design concept that you create. The plants are, of course, the crowning glory but are not an end unto themselves. By designing the physical aspects of the garden first your selection of plants will evolve as part of a consistent whole.

First draw an accurate scaled plan of your garden and plot in all the existing features. Next take a sheet of paper and answer the following:

1 Have you studied the internal colours and materials and furniture styles of the rooms that look onto the garden?
2 Have you studied the external colours and materials of your house, e.g. bricks, windows, doors?
3 Which room(s) overlook the garden? Drawing room? Family room? Dining room? Kitchen?
4 Does your garden slope or would you like to create split levels?
5 Is natural site drainage a problem?
6 What are your favourite colours?
7 Have you carried out a pH test on the soil?
8 What sort of plants and shrubs are you most fond of?
9 Are you a keen gardener or can you afford someone to carry out garden maintenance?
10 Are you prepared only to do simple garden chores?
11 Are you likely to grow your own vegetables? Do you want a separate garden or will you intermingle the vegetables with the plants?

12 Is your garden overlooked and from which angle?

13 Are there any buildings, pylons, or other eyesores that can be seen from your garden which you wish to obscure?

14 Apart from the house itself is there alternative access to your garden?

15 Do you have a balcony or do your upper rooms look down onto the garden?

16 Which aspect does your garden face and where does the sun last longest and least?

17 At what time do you use your garden? Breakfast, lunch, dinner, evenings or weekends?

18 Which existing features do you wish to retain or remove?

19 How old are your children and their friends? 0–3? 3–6? 6–11? 11 + ?

20 Are they keen on sport and if so which type of sport?

21 Do you or would you like to exercise in the garden. If so what type of exercise? Tennis, swimming, badminton, golf, croquet, cricket, etc.?

22 Do you entertain at home very often?

23 Do you entertain friends in the garden? If so how many on average? Maximum likely number?

24 How well, or little, do you get on with your neighbours?

25 Are there any marauding pets in the area?

26 Are there any outside services in difficult positions, e.g. drains, manhole covers, gas/electric/water points?

The answers to questions 1–5 will largely determine the type of garden you need and will go some way towards determining the overall theme.

Questions 6–11 determine the eventual flora with which to decorate the design and questions 12–14 will decide the structural planting requirements in keeping with the theme.

A reminder of the differing situations you may wish to exploit are given in questions 15–21, and the answers should be used to design either separate or linked areas. When considering question 19 remember that children grow up very fast and one must design for both existing and future requirements.

Measure your garden furniture and calculate the patio or entertainment space requirement when answering questions 22 and 23.

Answering questions 24 and 25 determines the type of boundary fencing, and question 26 is a reminder to plot and then plan around any difficulties that could arise from the siting of utilities.

Fine. You are now at the stage to select a garden theme and carry out all the necessary detailed planning. Take in all the aspects that this book offers and by majoring on your personal design solutions you will soon be ready to create your own Fitted Garden. Between us, perhaps, we can consign the rectangular lawn and herbaceous borders to the obscurity to which they belong.

2 · THE TRADITIONAL ENGLISH GARDEN ·

No book on garden design would be complete without a section on traditional English gardens. However, rather than dwell on the classic cottage garden which, in my experience, people prefer to look at rather than try to create themselves, I thought it might be interesting to include two very different styles of English gardens, both classic in their own right.

VICTORIANA REVISITED

I was fortunate enough to meet Peter Sutherland, a truly charming actor with the Royal Shakespeare Company who, in between his very busy life on stage, reincarnates property with his partner Alan Harris. Their current development is an enormous Victorian house which they are returning to

The wrought iron-work was made from the staircase balustrades from inside the house.

The gate was also created from staircase balustrading. Note how the path (photographed before tiling) curves slightly up to the house.

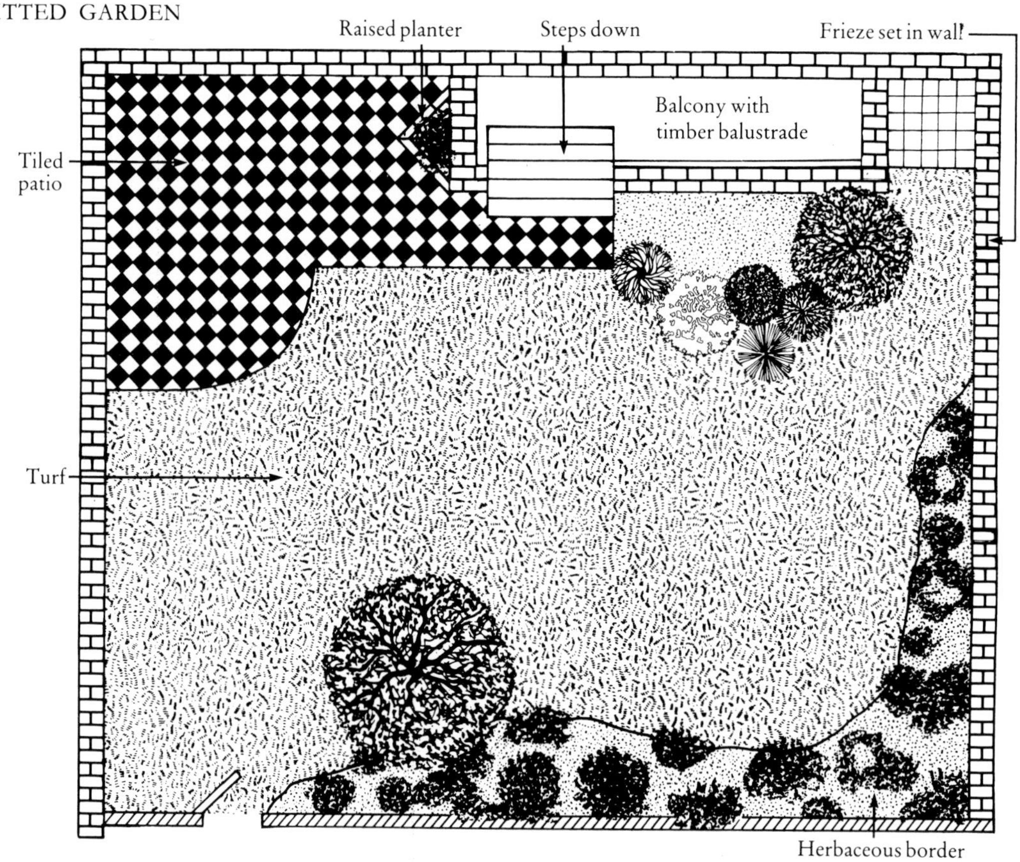

Fig. 1 *The garden complements the Victorian interior with the most notable theme features being the reclaimed Victorian tiles laid to the patio and the balustrading around the balcony.*

its former glory. When they first purchased the house, Peter determined that both the front and rear garden should be as 'Victorian' as possible and with some inspired recycling of Victorian junk by Alan they achieved two very attractive gardens in a relatively short time indeed. The house is seen from the road through a 1.2 m (4 ft) brick and wrought iron wall. The bricks, as one would expect are yellow stocks to match the house, whilst the wrought iron, and sheer genius this, is the original stair balustrading from inside the house. As you can see from the photograph the gate was specially designed to incorporate more of the balustrading. A coat of black paint and, voilà, Victorian railings!

The original path to the front door had to be replaced and Peter opted for a gentle curve in the new path. This is a very simple but effective device for increasing the visual dimensions of the garden and allows one to influence the observer's viewpoint to alternative attractions. In this particular garden, if the house was approached via a straight path it is unlikely that the columns that support the porch would be noticed. However, when approached obliquely one admires the borders which direct the eye to the columns, which, one recognizes with surprise, are Victorian gas lamp standards. Ingenious. Be careful with the curving path though. If it is overdone the postman and the newspaper boy will soon get fed up and will

Raised planter provides useful planting area next to the tiled patio.

create their own route to your front door, wearing out your carefully tended turf on the way.

The rear garden to this property is an absolute delight and once more is a combination of careful design, planting and recycled junk. Viewed from the rear of the garden the most striking feature is probably the small balcony which has been refurbished using ordinary wooden stair balustrading painted white. It provides a dramatic focal point whilst to the left the original conservatory provides additional colour from stained glass windows as well as the carefully tended flora inside. The adjoining garden wall is new, built from yellow stocks and has been considerably enhanced with the addition of some Victorian friezes of trade union crests taken from a building that was demolished. This kind of addition is always fun and provides an unexpected visual treat in what could have been a bland brick wall.

Another delight here is a huge old lawn roller which immediately conjures up images of ancient retainers striving to roll lush green lawns. Thank goodness for the modern motorized variety. The small patio has

Recently manufactured painted timber balustrades add authentic Victorian touch.

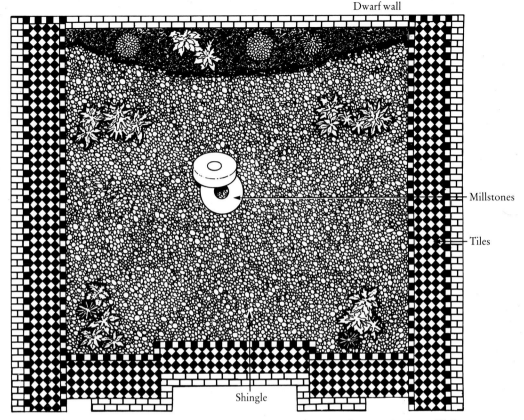

Dwarf wall

Millstones

Tiles

Shingle

Fig. 2 *Design for Victorian front garden featuring tiles and period millstones. Centre is filled with shingle as minimum maintenance alternative to turf. Millstones could be converted to water feature.*

been recreated using original paving tiles again recovered from a demolition site. The main planting considerations were for plants and shrubs that would grow relatively quickly and at the same time reproduce the visual effects of exotic plants on which our Victorian forebears were so keen. This has been achieved very effectively and I truly think Alan and Peter should open their garden to the public!

HOW HENRY MIGHT HAVE DONE IT

The ancient city of Southampton has much to recommend it. It is a bustling seaport and vigorous commercial centre. Furthermore, the City Fathers are unusually far sighted. One of their creations is the Tudor House Museum in Bugle Street which was built *c.* 1500 A.D. in the reign of Henry VIII. Between wars and wives Henry had the gardens at Hampton Court Palace created but these are a little large to try and recreate in mock-Tudor semi. However, down in Southampton a very clever lady, Sylvia Landsberg, has recreated a Tudor garden alongside the Museum with the help of finance from the City council and the Friends of the Museum. Sylvia Landsberg spent a great deal of time researching Tudor gardens and has largely managed to recreate the style and ambience of a private Tudor garden as well as stocking it with the type of flora available to the Tudor gardener.

Several features have been identified and created in the garden which again goes to prove that the 'fitted garden' concept of a total theme is very ancient indeed. As can be seen from the photographs and the plan (p. 20) the garden has been laid out to demonstrate the individual features as a part of an overall concept.

On entering the garden from the house one sees firstly the fountain plot. Considering the difficulties one has with modern plumbing products it comes as a constant source of surprise at just how innovative ancient gardeners were in diverting water sources to create pools and fountains. Certainly the copy of the medieval fountain demonstrated here does nothing to diminish this supposition.

To the left of the fountain is the charming 'secret garden' which in days of yore was termed the Privy Garden. Evidently no self-respecting

Excellent copy of medieval monastery's fountain.

sixteenth-century garden would be without one but whether this was because the boundary was marked originally by a privet hedge or because external lavatories were not yet common place is open to question. Whatever the answer to this conundrum the secret garden was used to protect rather more precious items and in Southampton a raised bed is shown as well as a bee skep positioned in a niche built expressly for this purpose 500 years ago.

In order to differentiate a Royal Garden from an ordinary country garden Henry VIII had heraldic beasts and striped railings incorporated into the design and this effect has been splendidly reproduced here, a nice idea that can be incorporated into a domestic pergola which also refutes the arguments of having non-'natural' colours in the modern garden. These railings were seen at Hampton Court originally and are testified to by a painting of 1545 and a bill for the work that still survives from 1533. The bill states 'Paid to Henry Blankeston for the painting of 96 pownchons white and green bearing up the rails at 12d the piece. Also paid to same for

Where the bee skeps . . . in the priory garden.

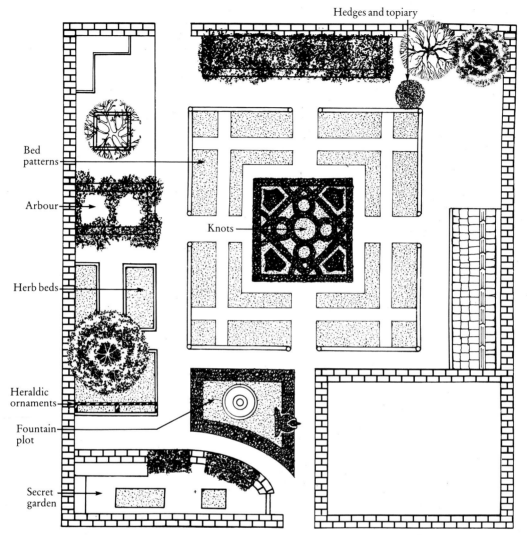

Hedges and topiary

Bed patterns

Arbour

Knots

Herb beds

Heraldic ornaments

Fountain plot

Secret garden

Fig. 3 *Sylvia Landsberg's faithful reproduction of Tudor theme garden in Southampton, England.*

like painting of 960 yards of rail white and green price the yard 6d.' Which just goes to show—landscaping was more expensive in Tudor times.

Herb beds have been a feature of gardens since Roman times and were used to grow vegetables and herbs for both food and medicine. Beds were raised to facilitate drainage by either mounding the soil up or surrounding them with boards.

Past the herb bed is another major feature, the arbour. In this garden it has been made from steel because of the advantages of maintenance but original flexible poles of ash, hazel or yew would have been tied together to make an enormous 'basket' interlaced with the common climbers of the time. And in those days vines were common-place.

Orchards would be used to create the major part of a Tudor garden and as well as apple, pear and cherry, mulberry, medlar, quince and fig would have been grown.

A parapet or mount was a common feature and used perhaps on the coast as a lookout point as here or perhaps to spot game in the larger estates.

Covered walks were very much a feature of these times as a shady spot or to plot in privacy. They were copied from the Continent and might have been a specifically designed frame to support climbers or could have been trees trained to grow as an arch. The third alternative was to use poles similar to those in the arbour.

Part of the fitting of Tudor gardens was to create a series of squares in the garden making up the whole. Royal gardens in France of this period had up to forty of these squares each the size of the entire Southampton plot. A typical small garden might have one such square but would also have paths crossing it thus cutting the original into quarters. The paths would typically be made from close packed sand or gravel and a railing or low hedge would surround them. Within the surround the beds would be planted in a symmetrical fashion with either one species or plant groups

Fig. 4 *Notable Tudor features include striped railings and herring-bone brickwork. Modern house bricks are much larger than in Tudor times. For better authenticity try to buy undersize bricks.*

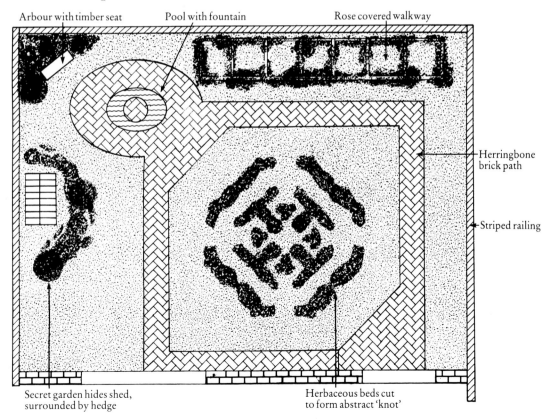

Arbour with timber seat

Pool with fountain

Rose covered walkway

Herringbone brick path

Striped railing

Secret garden hides shed, surrounded by hedge

Herbaceous beds cut to form abstract 'knot'

with similar needs. A second type of pattern was created using intricate strips of turf or herbs giving the appearance of a dwarf maze. The third pattern used is the most famous of all, the Elizabethan 'knot'.

The Elizabethan knot was essentially a bed with interlaced herb hedges. Accordingly, Sylvia Landsberg says about garden knots 'It shows all aspects of the Tudor character – love of decoration, contrivance, double meaning, hard work and nature well bridled.' The knot pattern at Tudor House is one of the smallest that can be made and is similar to the one carved on the doors of Tudor House. Sylvia Landsberg poses the question that this design may well conceal a trick, in that it could be said to resemble the four interlocking Coats of Arms of the City of Southampton.

Finally, it must be said that hawthorn, privet or sweetbriar were more commonly used in Tudor topiary as opposed to clipped box or yew. To the Tudors the latter were associated with death!

Congratulations are to be made to Sylvia Landsberg for creating this garden and, should you perhaps not wish to recreate your own Tudor garden, I would still recommend a visit to Southampton for the inspiration one will undoubtedly derive from it.

3 · C O U R T Y A R D S ·

Few people have true courtyards any more and almost anyone who has a small walled garden with a few cracked paving stones refers to it deprecatingly as the 'yard'. Usually courtyards are identical in that they are limited in size, there is little sunlight and no one feels it is worthwhile spending money on such a forlorn space. However, it is in areas like these that the designer's art is truly stretched. What can be done with this cracked concrete, this dank corner?

First, one must answer several questions if a successful creative solution is to be found. Is the courtyard to be used or is it really a thoroughfare from one part of the house to another? Can it be seen from rooms in the house and if so, are these rooms reception, dining or utility?

For example, if the courtyard is a passageway or if it is merely observed from a corridor inside the house, then the simplest and most effective solution is to position an unusual shrub or piece of sculpture which is seen almost in passing. As an alternative to the normal conservative concrete sculpture found in garden centres, one might like to try designing a timber sculpture which is fixed at eye level with a suitable climber trained over it. Yet another alternative, again suspended at eye level, might be a tree branch stripped of its bark and varnished to give it a gleaming pale finish. The main point is that this sculpture, although static, will visually 'move' as you walk past, and probably make you go back for a second look.

The same design parameters apply to a courtyard as they do for a large garden. If your courtyard is overlooked from a reception room then the visual effect should be predominately concerned with the activity normal in that room. Taken to its logical conclusion this would mean a waterfall outside every ground floor bathroom in the country (and why not?) but the point is not to have an 'active' garden that is viewed from, say, a drawing room that is used mainly for discovering a little quietude amongst the hurly burly. In the evening a still lit pool would be infinitely superior to a gushing waterfall immediately outside your drawing room windows.

THE TROUBLE WITH TREES

Mr and Mrs Schwab have the sort of garden, and the same sort of problems, that many new home owners are confronted with. When the properties were being constructed the developer, quite rightly, left some of the original trees standing on the site. Whilst this adds instant maturity it does

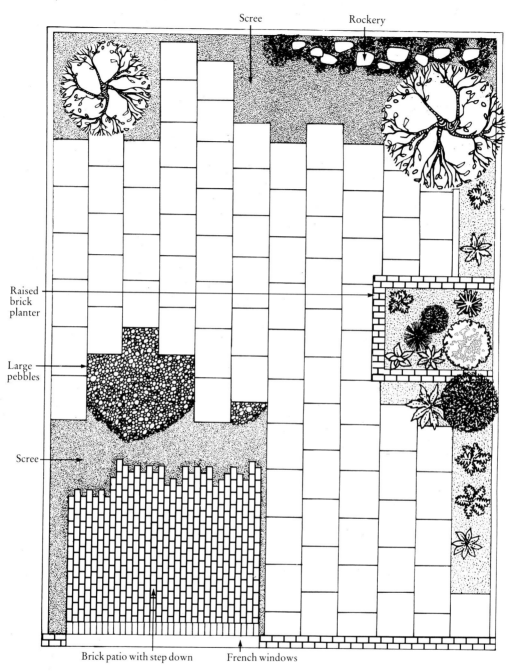

Scree

Rockery

Raised
brick
planter

Large
pebbles

Scree

Brick patio with step down

French windows

Fig. 5 *Planned to alleviate the maintenance problem of falling pine needles, the hard surfacing was selected to form a harmonious integration of differing colours and textures.*

Opposite: Hard surface colours complement the room with the view

give the annual 'fall'. With deciduous trees the difficulties are not quite as serious as larger leaves are decidedly easier to collect, but in a small courtyard sporting a tiny piece of turf, pine needles are a major nuisance. The solution undertaken can be used for a courtyard or for a larger patio design. The plot was approximately 11 m × 5.5 m (35 ft × 18 ft) wide, fenced on all sides and originally had a small patio constructed from conventional paving flags; a small lawn with herbaceous border completed the generally unexciting ensemble. Bob Schwab wanted a solution to the pine needle problem, and being interested in design generally as well as plants specifically also sought ideas for differing levels, surfaces and textures (Fig. 5).

The property is in the centre of a terrace and thus all the materials had to be carried by hand through the house with no access for construction

machinery. Add to this the fact that the garden was solid clay under the surface topsoil and one quickly realizes that major alterations to the site levels were out of the question.

For those of you who live in terraced property and are contemplating major reconstruction of your garden, add 20 per cent to your estimates. Materials handling through the house is very expensive in labour terms and if the labour is on an overtight budget you may find wheelbarrows have a nasty habit of bumping into internal walls and doors with an even greater cost by the end of the job.

The main view on to the garden was from the kitchen/diner and when one was seated at the dining room table the right-hand side of the garden was not completely visible.

The remedy for the pine needles was to pave the entire area with height differential introduced by constructing a rectangular planter from yellow

Potted plants traverse the garden, bring focus to raised planter and give added width dimension.

stock bricks to a height of 60 cm (2 ft). The planter is sited midway down the right-hand side for had it been sited on the left it would have been seen directly from the dining room and would have severely foreshortened the view. The second ploy used to give an illusion of depth is the rockery. The stone used here was selected for its creamy colour which toned with the man-made 'Yorkstone' paving slabs. The materials handling problem reared its head once more with the building of the rockery. Because there was no access for a forklift or an excavator the rocks had to be manhandled and thus the size of each piece was perforce restricted. However, the planting disguised this defect and as you can see from the photograph the final effect is very pleasing.

A large patio, or as in this case, a courtyard, can look very plain if a wide expanse of stone is laid with no thought given to overall form or shape. In this example we used brick paviors to emphasize texture and contrast.

Pebbles in right foreground give colour and textural relief between paviors and slabs. Rockery attracts the eye and increases visual depth.

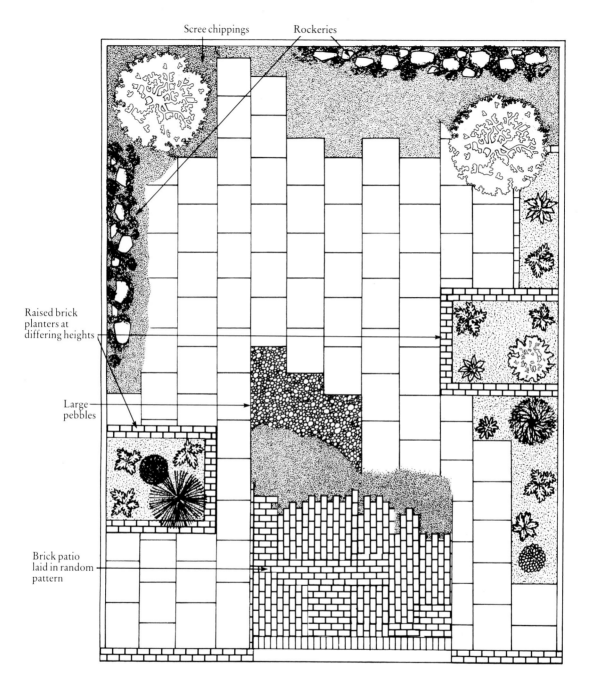

Scree chippings   Rockeries

Raised brick
planters at
differing heights

Large
pebbles

Brick patio
laid in random
pattern

Fig. 6 *A few simple changes will transform the tenor of this courtyard. I have assumed the French windows are now central and thus two different planters can be built with rockeries to balance the layout. The random pattern of the brick patio would give the feeling of a much older, more country style.*

Paviors are more hardwearing than brick and are less susceptible to frost damage. The particular pavior we specified was designed to be used on a concrete bed with mortar joints. As a clay subsoil has a tendency to dry out and crack in periods of prolonged hot dry weather a firm base is advisable for this type of pavior. If the base is insufficient the paviors will move and come winter water will seep beneath the mortar and the frost will then cause even more movement. Paviors of this type have an added advantage when working on a terraced site. As they are only half the thickness of conventional bricks, materials handling is reduced by 50 per cent.

Finally we chose to separate the paviors from the slabs with an intermediate colour and texture break provided by large (50–75 mm, 2–3 in diameter) pebbles. The pebbles range in colour from cream to dark blue and thus link both the red and dark purple of the paviors to the creamy buff of the slabs.

When photographed the garden was in its second season and looks surprisingly mature. The impression of maturity is obviously heightened by the trees but it is helped along by the colours used in the hard landscaping and by the instant colour from the potted plants.

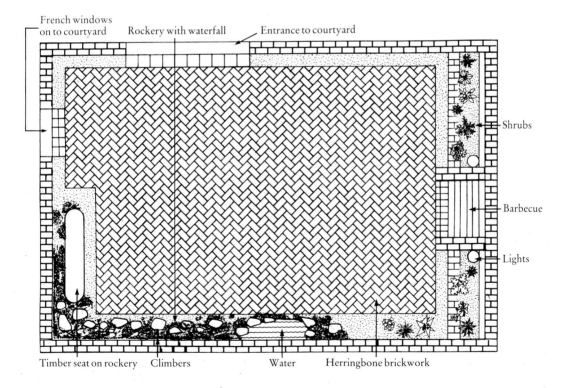

Fig. 7 *A small courtyard design predominated by herringbone paving is brought into focus by a waterfall bubbling down a rock face. The barbecue is illuminated for night time entertainment.*

MAINTENANCE AND MR MORRIS

Wayne Morris is a very successful restaurateur who also owns a catering company that takes him abroad for several months each year. His prime requirement in his garden was absolute minimum maintenance, followed by the need for sufficient room in which to entertain.

The garden was walled on each side and was originally a standard laid-to-lawn with herbaceous borders type. Wayne was fortunate in that his garden was surrounded by mature trees which gave attractive colour and visual dimensions. The garden is viewed from the kitchen window and through small French doors in the sitting room. A natural style was wanted and given that the house was built from the ubiquitous London yellow stocks

Yellow stock brick path demands attention and takes view from sitting-room to the mandatory – for a restauranteur – barbecue. Barbecue design incorporates preparation area as well as fire, and has storage for garden tools etc. underneath.

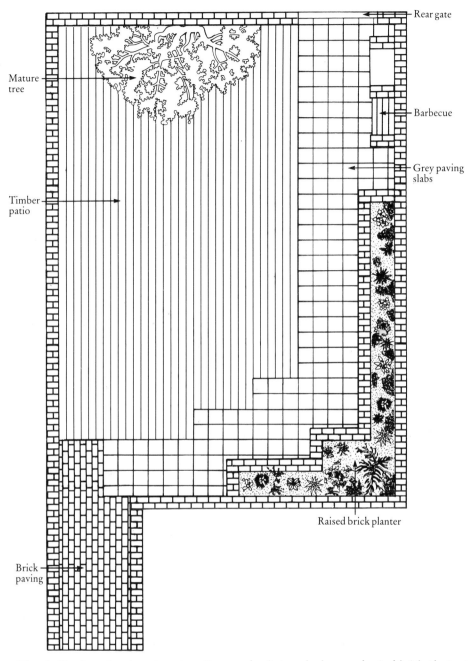

Rear gate

Mature
tree

Barbecue

Grey paving
slabs

Timber
patio

Raised brick planter

Brick
paving

Fig. 8 *De rigeur for the restaurateur. Rear garden features barbecue and raised brick planter to match.*

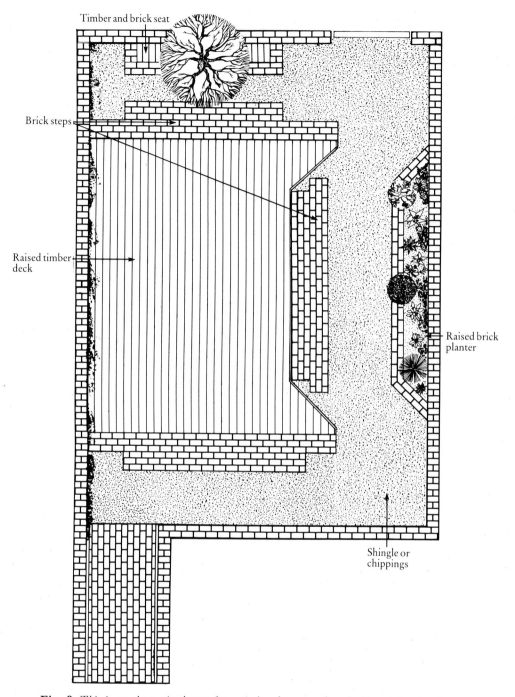

Timber and brick seat

Brick steps

Raised timber deck

Raised brick planter

Shingle or chippings

Fig. 9 *This is an alternative layout for a timbered courtyard, and although the shingle may provide a home for a few airborne weeds, it would be less expensive than paving the entire area.*

View from kitchen window on to raised timber patio. The window will eventually be framed by climbers from planter built below.

rendered in grey painted cement to the first floor windows, both our colour and material usage was therefore defined in advance: yellows, greys and derivations thereof.

It was decided that a slightly raised natural timber deck would provide an interesting visual feature especially as it would be positioned directly under a tree with the obvious mental link (see Fig. 8). The raised patio is the main feature seen from the kitchen windows. The majority of the paving was planned as grey riven slabs which also helped to give clean symmetrical lines to the finished design. As one would expect from a restaurateur, a barbecue was built in and we decided to use a natural Indian stone for the barbecue servery. This stone, called *kotah*, polishes up well and also has large areas of fossilized plants within it. A most unusual and attractive stone indeed but unfortunately it is generally too expensive to be used as paving. Following our initial thoughts on a fairly geometrical approach, we also included some raised planters built in yellow stocks and similarly laid a walkway in brick to contrast with the grey paving slabs. The positioning of the planters was carefully planned with regard to the views. The path as seen in the photograph invites the observer out of the sitting room towards a planter and on to the raised patio, whilst an additional planter was sited outside the kitchen window. Climbers are trained from here to trellising fixed to the rear of the property and eventually the view from the kitchen will be framed with flowers.

One must take great care when designing or building close to the house not to bridge the damp-proof course. If it is not possible to build the retaining wall separately, then render the house wall with a sand and cement finish mixed with a waterproofing agent, and then apply a damp-proof membrane. Before the membrane dries out throw some more sand on it as a key and then put on an additional coat of waterproofed rendering. Regrettably I have seen too many examples of rising damp caused through inexpert gardeners disregarding this most basic tenet.

4 · ORIENTAL GARDENS ·

To produce a true rendition of a Japanese garden needs years of careful study but perhaps a brief background to the Oriental arts may help the reader who wishes to use the Orient as inspiration for design.

Principally, and I apologize to the purists in advance, inspiration for Japanese gardens is drawn from four sources. Lack of space, China, tea and religion.

Japan is blessed with some of the most awe-inspiring natural landscapes in the world. Soaring mountain vistas, volcanoes, an abundance of water and waterfalls, forests both pine and deciduous and, of course, the ever present groves of bamboo. Unfortunately, amongst all these rocky mountains there is little space for either food cultivation or people and thus the Japanese art of miniaturization was born. To waste land for merely decorative purposes was originally the pursuit of the rich, for the Japanese peasant of the Middle Ages had neither time nor land to devote to the cultivation of flora.

With a relatively large population and very little living space the Japanese of neccessity developed a highly ritualized society in which, for example, two families living on either side of a paper wall would pretend not to hear one another's conversation. These rituals first became codes of etiquette and then codes of honour which were so deeply ingrained in the Japanese psyche that failure to observe the rules of conduct could result in social banishment or worse. This ritualization, under the Zen philosphy, eventually became part of most Japanese art forms.

Although Japan was closed to the outside world for centuries trade was continued with its largest neighbour, China, for a considerable period. Japanese art developed from China during the Heian period in the eighth century AD and I feel that the earliest Chinese influences from meditation to macrobiotic menus are all-pervading, albeit developed along more pure and aesthetic lines.

The British invented their own tea ceremonies, and to a degree accompanying art forms, but the formality and style are as nothing in comparison with the Japanese *cha-yoriai* or 'tea-meeting' perfected five or more centuries earlier. *Cha* was originally introduced to Japan from China by a Zen priest named Eisai in the twelfth century when it was used in the Zen monasteries to keep the monks awake during their periods of meditation. By the fourteenth century the 'tea-gathering' was established

Daitoku Ji Temple, Kyoto, Japan. Moss replaces grass, minimizes maintenance. Stark lines softened by 'water', raked gravel swirls up to and around moss islands and to sentinel rocks standing guard at temple entrance.

Opposite: Entrance to tea house, Kanzani, Japan. Screen and roof line frame flaming autumn colours as only the Japanese seem to do.

among most classes in Japan and especially by the feudal lords. The upper class gatherings soon became more than tea appreciation societies and the hardware itself, the best still came from China, also had to be taken careful note of. As time passed special rooms, called *shoins*, were developed and in most cases were extravagantly decorated but, as in all things, the designers, and in this case it was more Zen philosophers, thought they could do better. Under the influence of philosophers/tea masters such as Murato Juko and Takeno Joo taking tea was refined into a ritualized observance of form, style and movement. The concepts of *Wabi*, literally the appreciation of 'quiet solitude' and *Sabi*, the enjoyment of 'tranquil, aged beauty' were introduced and then developed further by another tea master, Se no Rikyu in the 1500s. The latter's contribution was to create the *soan chanoyu* or 'tea ceremony in a thatched hermitage' which led to the establishment of the tea houses which now project one of the lasting images of Japanese garden design.

The traditional imagery of Japan can still be seen today in and around the ancient city of Kyoto, the capital from 794 AD until 1869. Stands of bamboo drive up to the sky from a surface of rock and scree, the leaves in stylized silhouette against the traditional white of the tea houses.

By now you will have realized that Japanese garden design, so instantly recognizable in all its varied forms, is the result of centuries of development and, perhaps more than any other school of landscaping thought, is devoted to composition and balance. Nowhere is this more apparent than in the perfection of the dry landscape garden, the *kare-sansui*. Carefully raked sand is used to represent water and rocks and stones are positioned as mountains or waterfalls. However, the overall effect sought by the designer is not a realistic interpretation of nature but a formal presentation of symmetry, harmony and above all balance of composition.

As I have tried to point out, it has taken centuries of social development to create the Japanese style and whilst the Western mind admires it superficially, the subtler nuances are lost on most of us. However, this has not stopped designers taking inspiration from this most elegant and distinctive of styles.

THE BACKYARD ART OF ZEN

Today most people want gardens that are simple to maintain. Even mowing the lawn is becoming a lost art in the suburbs, and, frankly, quite rightly so. If your plot measures less than 50 sq.m (55 sq.yards) maintaining a lawn in the middle of it is probably caused by lack of design forethought rather than the desire for recherché rolling pastures. You need to mulch, mow, roll, aerate, feed, weed and generally give such care and attention that writers get rich just explaining how to do it.

Rather than a lawn, consider the Japanese method of training various types of moss over shingle or rock. This provides the requisite greenery with none of the maintenance. What about somewhere to sit? Easy: one designs raised areas of natural timber or stone within the overall area.

The photograph on p. 41 demonstrates a simplified form of a Japanese theme created for a development of town houses for Taylor Woodrow Homes Ltd, in Park Royal, London. The executives at Taylor Woodrow are innovative and far sighted, none more so than the Sales Director, Tom Fairclough. In 1984 Tom accepted my suggestion of 'The Fitted Garden' in that the one thing new homes generally lacked was a landscaped rear garden. Accordingly we designed a range of gardens that a new home buyer could select and have created for them before they moved in (see opposite and p. 40). It is largely due to Tom's foresight that many new home buyers

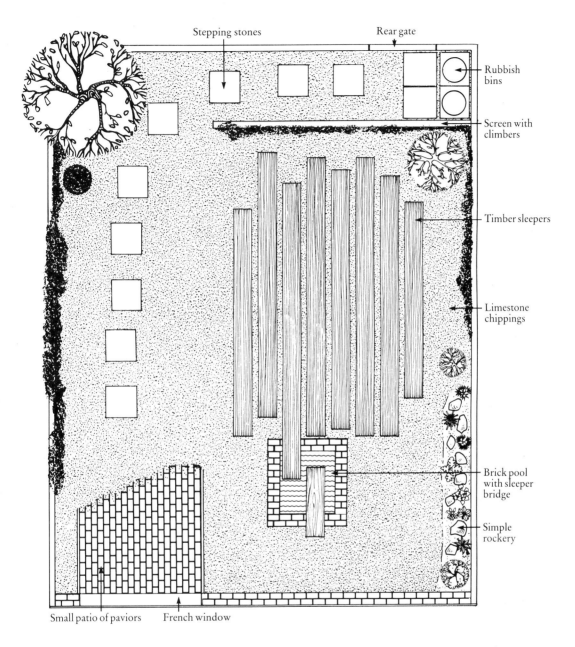

Fig. 10 *This design was built for a Taylor Woodrow show house in Park Royal, London, and was the first commercial 'Fitted Garden'.*

in the United Kingdom now have this facility offered to them as a standard package; other builders soon copied the idea.

The disadvantage of 'packaging' a range of designs is that one has no clear idea of the eventual purchasers' taste. For instance, is the client likely to be a purist or would they not have any idea of Zen Buddhism? At the Park Royal site the purchaser profile of the likely buyers was young marrieds or middle level executive singles. If married they would both be

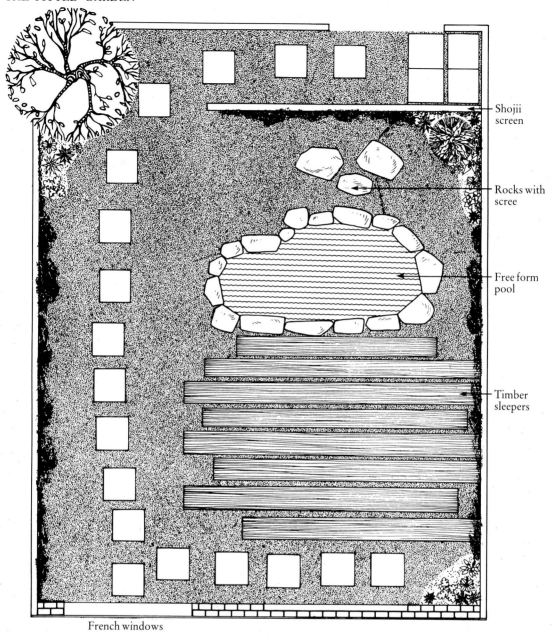

Shojii
screen

Rocks with
scree

Free form
pool

Timber
sleepers

French windows

Fig. 11 *An alternative water feature and different layout for the timber sleepers once more changes the entire vista. This style is deliberately less formal than a strictly Zen approach and is more in keeping with British 'wa'.*

working and unlikely to have children. It might well be their first home and in any case they were unlikely to stay in the house for more than three years. We decided to take the lowest common denominator and produce an Anglicized version of a Japanese theme. We took three elements of Japanese design, rock, water, and timber, looked at their English counterparts and then decided how these might be most enjoyed by a householder. It was obvious from the purchaser profile that the buyers would not have a great deal of time to spend on actual gardening. Minimum maintenance was a priority.

The budgets we were working to precluded the use of more exotic shingles and we decided to use grey limestone chippings which contrasted pleasantly with the dark red of the house bricks and the Blockley paviors used for the tiny patio adjacent to the patio doors. When wet, limestone chippings have the added advantage of changing colour to a very soft damask pink. The paviors were laid on a sand base with the outer perimeter mortared on to footings. The paviors were laid in a random pattern and were allowed to 'drift' into the chippings. The chippings themselves were purchased in two size gradings which, when spread, were again allowed to 'drift' into each other providing an image of wind blowing across the surface of water. Normally speaking the gravel surface would be raked into specific patterns but this, we felt, would be too severe (and maintenance intensive) for the British homebuyer.

Japanese-style garden designed for Taylor-Woodrow Homes Ltd, showing close-up of pool and use of timber sleepers.

In Japanese gardens timber also plays a large role so we decided to use timber railway sleepers as a second patio and also to provide a bridge over the rectangular pool. Given the amount of shingle in the garden it was inevitable that stones would be kicked into the pool if we had created a 'natural' effect; pragmatism pointed to a brick surround.

A timber screen was added to conceal dustbins and the like with a variety of clematis trained over it and finally stepping stones were included to guide the eye through the garden and beyond the screen giving the impression of further concealed vistas.

A garden like this is immediately identifiable as a Japanese theme but with good British compromise overlaid upon it. It is practical in that the planting is very simple and mainly restricted to specimen shrubs for impact and year-round colour; moreover, the basic layout will fit into a myriad of garden shapes and sizes.

ONCE UPON A WALK...

We were commissioned to refurbish the rear half of a mature garden that backed onto a railway line. The main problem was that the limestone scalpings used in the construction of the track leached into the garden and made it very difficult to grow limestone hating shrubs such as rhododen-

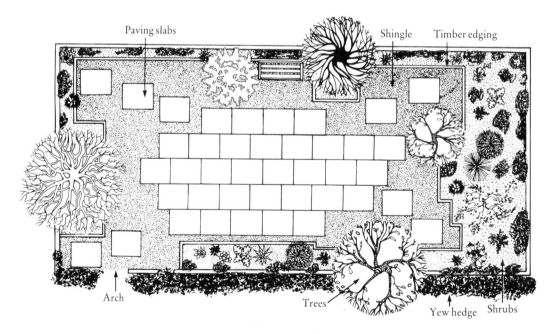

Fig. 12 *As an extension of an existing traditional English garden, a dramatically different approach was required. This Japanese style design satisfied this need, and endless interpretations can be created.*

A secret Japanese-style garden lies beyond the English arch.

drons. Sharp-eyed readers will have noticed that in the previous garden we had planted rhododendrons in among limestone scalpings. Here is the secret. We excavated a trench around the planting area and packed it with peat to neutralize the acidity. It is both expensive and labour-intensive, but it works.

Our client wanted a secret garden that would be 'happened upon' while walking in the traditionally English part of the plot. The section we were working on was separated from the main garden by a box hedge and although extremely overgrown contained a variety of fruit trees: apple, plum and cherry. Given the spring blossoms, it cried out for a Japanese treatment. Once cleared the site appeared relatively large for a secret

Paved patio floats in scree sea, stepping stones lead from entrance to points of interest.

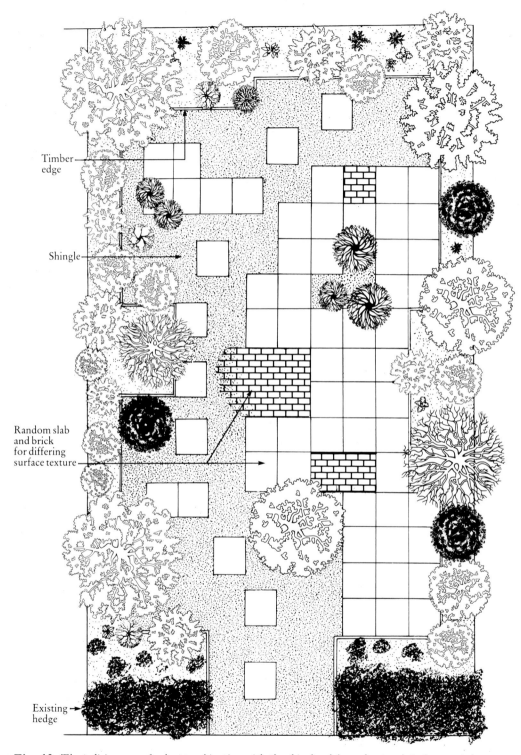

Timber edge

Shingle

Random slab and brick for differing surface texture

Existing hedge

Fig. 13 *The judicious use of colour combination with the shingle, slabs and natural timber created an entirely different mood at the far end of a traditional English garden. The existing trees provide a soothing dappled effect in summer.*

Right: Quiet corner features owner's Japanese vase with interesting mask (Venetian?) top right. Good example of introducing art to plain brick wall.

Below: Two distinctive rockery styles.

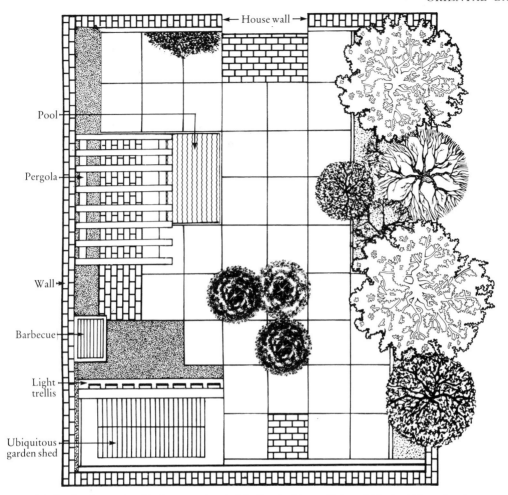

Pool

Pergola

Wall

Barbecue

Light trellis

Ubiquitous garden shed

House wall

Fig. 14 *In this design the ubiquitous garden shed is disguised by trellising which should be painted to harmonize with the pergola. For a Chinese influence try black, red and gold.*

garden, being approximately 6 × 6 m (20 × 20 ft). A further requirement was that having discovered the garden one would need somewhere to sit and enjoy the blossoms.

We decided to give the overall design a random symmetry which, one realizes, sounds like a total contradiction of terms. It was achieved, however, by designing the surrounding borders as a series of rectangles which complimented the random layout of the paved area. Designing a random pattern is actually a fairly difficult task and one needs to draw it to scale and then physically lay the slabs dry to ensure the selected pattern does not repeat, and, more importantly in a restricted area, that it fits with the minimum amount of slab cutting.

The borders, already trenched and filled with peat were separated from the chippings by treated timber gravel boards which, in turn, emphasized the rectangular aspects of the garden. This secret garden is dramatically different from the rest of the plot; stepping through the entrance by the box hedge is like being transported 2000 miles. Try it for yourself.

5 · S P L I T   L E V E L S ·

One normally finds a garden split into levels when the actual plot slopes and the home owner finds pushing the mower up-hill too much of a task. Tons of topsoil are transported from one side of the site to another until what was once an interesting topography becomes the conformist bowling green so beloved by the British.

A more interesting alternative, perhaps, is to design and construct plateaux within the context of the predominant slope and thus create interesting grottos, rock 'outcrops' or the natural timber decks that our antipodean and American cousins do so well.

The other, but more rare, situation in which split levels occur is when a creative home owner becomes bored with a garden laid mainly to lawn to use the estate agent's jargon (i.e. flat with herbaceous borders), and decides to alter the levels to increase the visual dimensions of the property. This type of garden is usually more original in concept as the designer is deliberately and consciously attempting to liberate the levels and rise above the norm.

DRY STREAMS ADD DRAMA

When we were first commissioned to regenerate this garden (see Fig. 15) a small patio existed at the rear of the house and was viewed from the kitchen and French windows in the drawing room.

The patio was too small for all but the minimum of table and chairs and was confined to this space because of the steep bank that the original developers had left. For London and the suburbs the garden was relatively large being approximately 90×18 m (300×60 ft) and contained a few mature lilac trees and unspectacular shrubs planted in narrow beds on either side of a rectangular lawn. The far end of the south-facing garden was usually in shade from a mixed stand of mature deciduous and coniferous trees. In short, a fairly ordinary suburban garden.

The brief was basically to extend the patio, provide a focal point, and produce more visual width to the plot.

It is my view that a view from a drawing room should be relaxing but relatively static. The initial suggestion of adding a waterfall and stream to run down the steep bank that led from the patio was discarded for two reasons.

Firstly, on this site, the inclination of the slope was away from the house

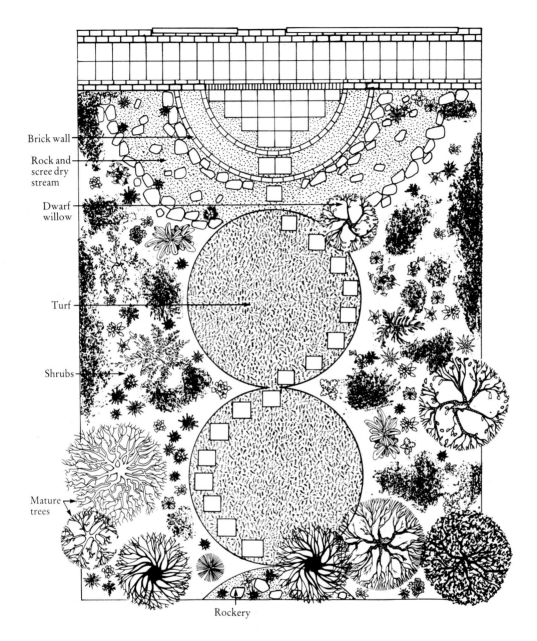

Brick wall

Rock and
scree dry
stream

Dwarf
willow

Turf

Shrubs

Mature
trees

Rockery

Fig. 15 *A large garden with a requirement for minimum maintenance. Dry stream provides the source of inspiration.*

and therefore the waterfall would have needed a header pool or spring, gurgling, somewhat unnaturally, out of the patio. Moreover, it would only have been seen from the far end of the garden as you look towards the house.

Secondly, given my view that the room with the view defines the garden elements, then moving water would have disturbed the equilibrium of the drawing room.

49

Stark boulders highlighted
with splash of colour ...
dry streams add drama.

As a compromise the solution to providing additional interest to the site was met by designing a dry stream at the base of the terrace. Having fixed on a concept of a curving stream then the remainder of the design came together fairly quickly.

The drop from the existing patio level was approximately 1.5 m (5 ft) and would therefore require six steps as a comfortable rise on a staircase is between 18–23 cm (7–9 in). The terrace, now rather grander than a patio, was brick built to co-ordinate with the texture and colour of the house bricks and this in itself rather determined that the terrace would be formal in style.

To alleviate the formality the terrace was conceived as a series of semi-circles (see opposite, top, and p. 49) with the surface made more interesting by using a combination of shingle and plain riven slabs. Additional advantages of saving costs within the budget were gained as it negated cutting the slabs to fit the curves and also had the effect of blending the dry stream with the paved area.

Bringing the beds into the foreground shortens the visual length of the garden and makes the eye traverse across the width rather than the length. This factor, in combination with the focal point of the dry stream has the overall effect of broadening the aspect.

Left: Conceived as series of semi-circles. Terrace levels drop to dry stream below.

Below: Dwarf willow, *right foreground*, enhances illusion of stream bed.

The shingle for the stream was laid upon an 8 cms (3 in) bed of dry mixed sand and cement which provides a firm sub-surface and helps to control unwanted weed development. Rocks were selected by colour and size to co-ordinate with the paving and the close-up shows how smooth boulders, rather than rocks, were used within the stream to suggest the erosion of water.

As to planting, what is more natural than a graceful willow arching over water? This particular variety is a weeping dwarf, which was positioned to be seen from the drawing room.

Since the solution to the split level garden was a series of semi-circles, the shape of the lawn was a foregone conclusion, but it was during this relatively simple phase of the refurbishment that disaster struck. The planner in charge of the scheme had used architect's drawings to determine the garden size and had not physically checked the dimensions. The garden plan showed three circular lawns linked by stepping stones but when the time came to recut the borders we were about 11 m (36 ft) short. Frantic revisions, not to mention recriminations, ensued and the compromise was a semi-circular lawn at the farthest end of the garden which disappears into the trees and rockery. In retrospect the compromise is actually a nice design point for it gives the impression of the circle continuing into the woods beyond the boundary.

The point of this admission, however, is never to trust an architect's plans. Furthermore, always lay out your design with string or twine so that any problems can be anticipated and overcome before the first shovel bites into the sod.

When this garden matures the final effect will have dramatic impact. The banks of the dry stream will be softened by planting and the specimen shrubs and trees will line the banks just as one would find in nature. The planting in the curved beds will fill out and soften the precise circles and finally leave the impression of a series of glades which invite the observer into the woods beyond.

HERBACEOUS HIGH RISE

A one in two rise in your backgarden would give many people palpitations but where developers build, designers follow. It would be nice if the developers asked designers' opinions first, but who are we to argue with a chronic land shortage and a few bucks to be made?

This particular site is on a very well planned development in Wimbledon and the charming owner, Mr Roger Penny, is, as you can see, a keen plantsman.

The plot was untouched when I first saw it, just the normal builder's rubble. The main problem was that access was restricted through the house which was, as you have correctly guessed, newly carpeted.

Paving, brickwork, shingle, boulders, all harmonize within the circular design concept and develop the total theme.

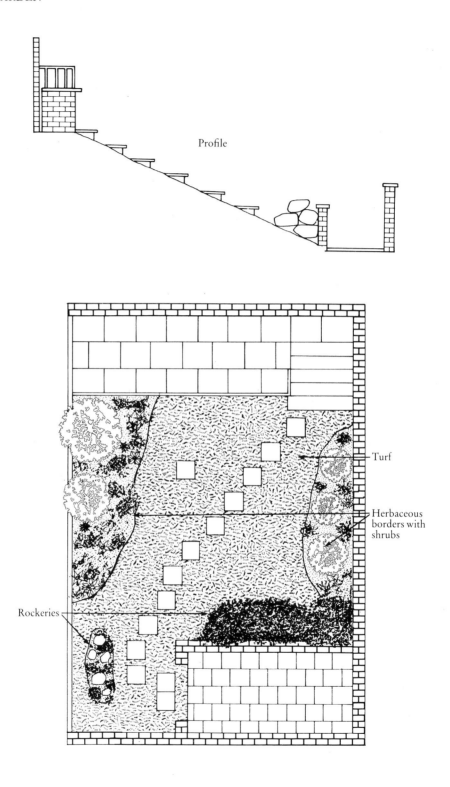

Profile

Turf

Herbaceous
borders with
shrubs

Rockeries

The extra tonnes of topsoil and other materials had to be manhandled over a 4 m (12 ft) wall at the bottom of the garden. No job for the fainthearted!

The existing raised patio was constructed by the developer and perched on a sheer cliff face of brickwork contained by a wrought iron balustrade. Our brief was simple in the extreme. Construct an additional patio and short of installing a cable car, find some way to move up and down the garden without causing a heart attack from over exertion. Fortunately our client was not daunted by the prospect of mowing the slopes of a mountain

Hover mowers are highy recommended when your turf takes on aspects of alpine pastures.

Fig. 16 (Opposite) *A simple but effective method to provide a second sun patio on a steeply sloping site.*

Foreshortened aerial shot shows straight lines of garden softened by curving beds and rockery leading to second patio.

and, having determined his love of plants we set about removing the rubble.

The garden measured approximately 11 × 4 m (36½ × 13 ft) but it must be remembered that these measurements were made on a very steep incline. Normally I try to allow a minimum area of 2.5 × 2.5 m (8¼ sq ft) for a patio, as this is sufficient room for a table and four to six chairs. If we had installed a patio of this size the severity of the slope would have needed a retaining wall some 1.5 m (5 ft) in height. As this would have had the combined effect of both unduly dominating the garden and leaving very little room for greenery the patio had to be scaled down to the space available.

An area of 3 sq m was finally excavated to levels and whilst most of the builder's rubble was disposed of the little topsoil that was usable was

Fig. 17 (Opposite) *The timber surrounds are the main feature of this method of laying a path on a steep slope. The combination of timber, rock, turf and alpine planting, together with the slope, is reminiscent of an alpine pasture.*

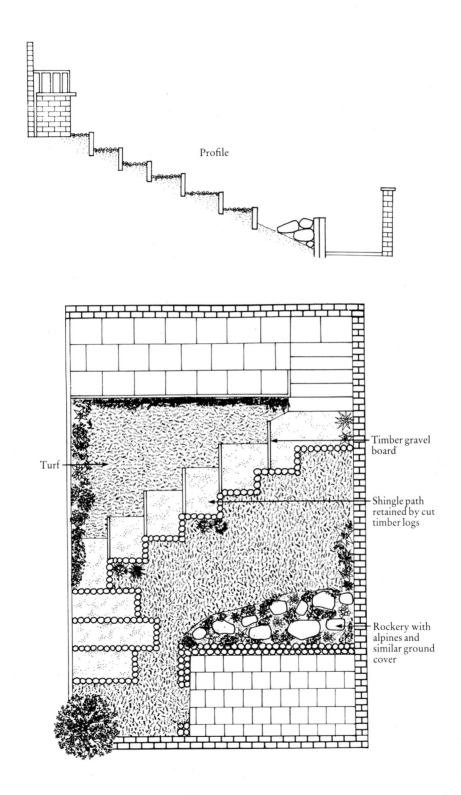

Profile

Turf

Timber gravel
board

Shingle path
retained by cut
timber logs

Rockery with
alpines and
similar ground
cover

retained for the rockeries. The retaining wall was built and then backfilled with some of the rubble and topped off with various grades of shingle (larger sizes first) to facilitate drainage. Similarly weepholes were introduced into base of the wall.

Responding to the requirement for a little bit of country in the midst of the metropolis we used oversized pitch faced blocks to give an air, however small, of rusticity. The blocks married in with the grey riven paving that the developer had used on the original patio and which we duplicated to form the surface of the steps and second patio.

The rockery was designed to encircle the steps as they led to a second patio and also to give the appearance of a natural outcrop; one might be forgiven for thinking the house was built on a massive rock face, sprinkled here and there with pockets of soil.

An alternative to steps when faced with a steep rise is a shingle path retained by natural wood or split logs. However, walking down such a

Patio will eventually be screened by planting.

Tiny, triangular London garden with split-level treatment.

path, especially in high heels, is quite a balancing act. On this site the added disadvantage would have been the loss of another 20 sq m of precious planting area and would have given the visual effect of a rustic helter skelter.

Finally, we plumped for paved steps set in a slight curve that led one from the top patio down and through the rock outcrop to the second patio. The steps were also set on pitch faced blocks.

Another problem on steep sites is the leaching effect of rainwater on the topsoil. Over a period of time the soil and the inherent nutrients will move and to counteract this effect high density planting is a good idea.

One of the major reasons for the impact of this very small garden with its difficult site conditions is Robert Penny's highly original planting plan. There are vivid colours year round supported by masses of evergreens.

6 · WATER GARDENS ·

WATER, WHY NOT?

Water brings a garden alive. The sound, the movement in the sunlight or floodlit in the evenings, it is one of the crowning achievements of the landscaper's art; but pools, ponds and water features are a constant source of contention between designers, who normally love them, and their clients, who can find lots of reasons not to.

There are three main difficulties with pools. The first is position, the second is maintenance and the third is small children. If you position a pool under a tree then you must expect leaves to fall in it. The leaves rot, give off

Diving dolphins feature at the manufacturer's show garden in Northampton (Haddonstone Ltd.).

noxious elements and kill the fish. So, each fall, drape a fine nylon mesh across the water to catch the leaves and empty it when you do your normal garden chores. Oxygenating plants are readily available from most garden centres and similarly water snails will help keep the algae at bay. Ensure that there are sufficient of both and you will start to avoid the brackish mess that so many pools seem to generate. It is best to empty small garden pools annually, clean them out and refill them. If you do not wish to do it, get a maintenance gardener to do it for you. It should not take more than a day and it is a small price to pay for the delights of a water feature.

Another way around the problem is to build a waterfall with a sump hidden beneath the rocks. The water then circulates continuously but does not collect in surface pools. The Georgian water feature pictured here can also be used by allowing the water to fall into a pebble-filled sump.

Veritable school of dolphins in Georgian-style set piece.

Lion mask fountain flows into semi-circular pool.

If you are about to embark on landscaping your garden and have young children, then remember that the children grow up. Plan the pool into the overall design and construct it. Then fill it with play sand for use as a sandpit until the children are old enough to appreciate the possible dangers.

AN ELEGANT ESTATE IN EAST TWICKENHAM

Off a major trunk road in the busy London Borough of Richmond, a Victorian Developer built an estate of detached 'stockbroker' properties and had the foresight to decree that the nine acres in the middle of the area should remain in permanent trust and that it should be treated as a communal garden for the residents.

The result today is a small but extremely attractive park, abundantly stocked with mature trees and as a centre piece the charming lake that is shown in the photograph. Note the white painted wrought iron footbridge

Delightful Victorian wrought iron bridge. If your plot cannot support one this size, have it built in miniature.

that arches gracefully over the water and is reflected in still calm below. Whilst we were photographing a family of ducks paddled past and an inquisitive heron dropped by to investigate. Idyllic when one considers the unheard roar of the traffic is a mere 100 m away.

Few of us are lucky enough to own nine acres in which to landscape a lake but as water is such an important aspect for gardens it is nice to seek inspiration from our forebears. In your own garden you might like to consider the construction of a similar bridge, but in miniature. Try using the wooden balustrades normally found on staircases. These are available from better timber merchants and the same timber merchant might be able to make the handrail and supports for the bridge. If not, they should be able to put you in touch with a competent joiner.

The availability of polythene pool liners (which you can have made

Unheard roar of the traffic is a mere 100 metres away.

specifically to size) is widespread today and it means that anyone with a medium sized or larger type of garden can duplicate this beautiful Victorian park, albeit on a slightly smaller scale.

SLIGHTLY SURREAL IN SHEEN

The client for whom I designed this garden in Sheen is a gifted amateur sculptress and wanted a garden with absolutely minimum maintenance that would serve to highlight her work.

The plot is approximately 36×12 m (120×40 ft) and when I first saw it, the garden was a complete wilderness. At the rear of her large Edwardian house a small raised patio already existed but was beyond repair and at the end of this patio stood the ubiquitous wooden shed. Midway down the plot was a very soft and semi-permanent damp area covering the complete width

Stark pool complements pool-side lounger.

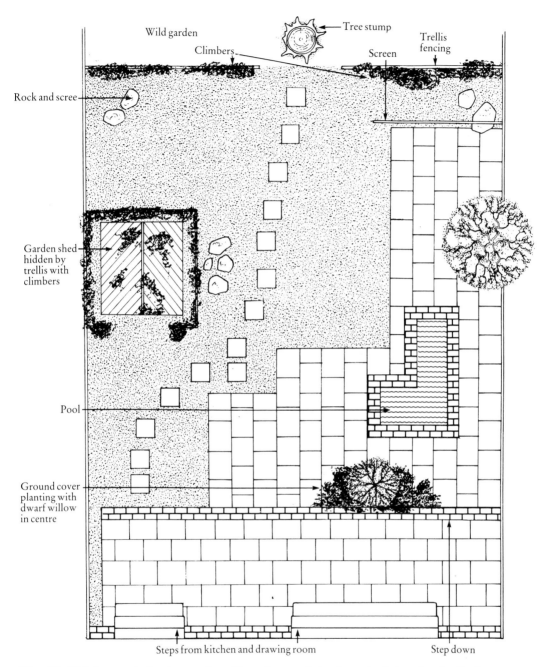

Wild garden

Climbers

Tree stump

Screen

Trellis fencing

Rock and scree

Garden shed hidden by trellis with climbers

Pool

Ground cover planting with dwarf willow in centre

Steps from kitchen and drawing room

Step down

Fig. 18 *Slightly surreal when in actuality, this garden was designed as a back-drop for the client's sculpture.*

of the garden which was quite possibly caused by a leaky pond installed by a previous owner. At the far end of the garden a large elm had been removed down to the stump.

Overall then, a long, fairly narrow garden with bad drainage, overlooked on all sides, featuring a singularly large and ugly tree stump. The view on to

Ground cover in foreground tumbles down steps into entertainment area and separates pool.

the garden is from French windows in the sitting-cum-family room and from a single French door in the kitchen. The family wanted to entertain in the garden and the existing patio line was too small for the requisite garden furniture.

The brief was to provide an entertainment area, opportunities throughout the garden to site the modernist style of sculpture and minimum maintenance.

To break up the narrow vista and to give a courtyard area in which to entertain it was decided to extend the patio on two levels and create a timber screen divider. Eventually this screen will be lightly covered with clematis. This was widely spaced when planted so that there will always be a view from the sitting room into the courtyard area and beyond, thus giving the observer the feeling of wider horizons (see Fig. 18).

The existing shed was moved to the left-hand side of the garden out of the direct view from the sitting room and was disguised with a trellis surround as support for more climbers. The hanging baskets were added as an afterthought but contribute strongly to the inner courtyard theme.

The pool itself was designed as an irregular but geometric shape to compliment the patio perimeter. This particular pool was brick built from London stocks to match the house construction and the 'brick-on-edge' finish is reminiscent of a traditional well.

Left: How to enhance a utilitarian shed.

Below: Screen provides additional angle of interest from which to view the pool.

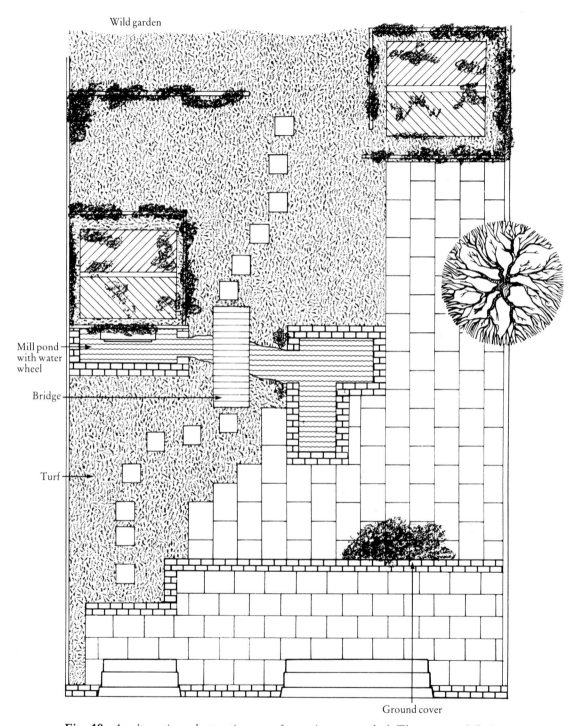

Wild garden

Mill pond
with water
wheel

Bridge

Turf

Ground cover

Fig. 19 *An alternative and attractive water feature is a water wheel. These are not difficult to construct, but as far as I am aware no-one is producing them commercially. In this case the ubiquitous shed could be painted to represent a mill or similar, but a coat of white paint and some pretty hanging baskets would give an 'olde worlde' effect.*

The minimum maintenance problem, which in this case previously meant mowing the lawn, was solved using shingle and creamy coloured rocks in a sparse, almost Japanese style. Because of the bad drainage, a sub-base of limestone scalpings was used, which, when compressed, formed a fairly solid surface hard enough to walk on without sinking while allowing surface drainage through minute holes.

Rocks were first selected for size, shape and colour and positioned individually. A peat-filled trench, to neutralize the lime which leaches from the scalpings, was dug around them. The scalpings were graded level to an overall depth of 75 mm (3 in) and then rolled before laying and grading the shingle. The plantings in and around the rockeries were mainly Ericae to provide year-round colour.

Finally, the stump! The tree surgeons had done the easy part of the job and had taken away the trees. Unfortunately the remaining stump was too small to facilitate a purchase and thence to pull it out and there was insufficient access to the garden to remove it by machine. These machines, incidentally, are aptly named Stump Gobblers! To remove the stump by

Rock and scree provide background for client's sculpture, with wild garden beyond.

digging and cutting would have cost almost as much as landscaping the entire garden so a cheap and effective solution had to be found.

We decided to partition this section with natural timber trellising and allow the area to grow *au naturel*. The stump itself was sanded to a smooth finish and will eventually be varnished and used as a dais for a life-size sculpture.

When photographed, the garden was in its second year and although it will take another four years to mature, it has, from its very inception, been a delight. As can be seen from the photographs, the overall creation with the outcropping rocks and expanse of shingle is somewhat ethereal and in combination with the sculptures produces a quality of surrealism. The still pool lit in the evening brings into focus the courtyard and entertainment area and lights interspersed in the rockeries and wild garden beyond provide the onlooker with a variety of tempting visual treats twelve months a year.

7 · R O C K   G A R D E N S ·

Everything considered, the rock garden represents the most difficult single challenge for a professional landscaper. It is not the movement of massive rocks, although more of this later. It is not the movement of tons of soil to regrade an escarpment. The problem is the armchair gardener reading books on rock gardens, and his subsequent disappointment when his mental image of the Massif Central is reduced to a 'currant bun' in his back garden.

Books specializing on rock gardens do, by their very nature, demonstrate mature rockeries: huge rocks, artfully placed, abundantly stocked with alpines flowing from every conceivable fissure and crevice. Unfortunately, it just isn't like that. What a specialist book does not demonstrate is the crane operator lifting the rocks into place. Or the JCB driver delivering a tonne of topsoil within a centimetre of the required position. Moreover, the photographs do not depict the driveway showing the access needed to get the machines on site to begin with.

What this book shows is what can reasonably be expected in a reasonably sized plot at a reasonable cost. This way, one avoids disappointments, slipped discs and a 'currant bun'.

Rocks are very heavy, which, one may feel, is a superfluous statement.

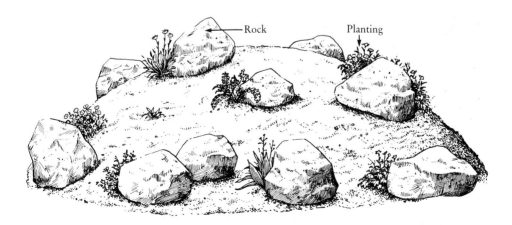

Fig. 20 *The usual currant bun is a heap of earth with rocks heaped on top. Unnatural. Avoid at all costs.*

This may be so, until one tries to move an inert object the size of a large pillow. Then one realizes that rocks are extremely heavy and are best left to the professionals. If you have restricted access to your property, and in planning a rockery this is the first consideration, then one must consider the size of rocks the access will allow; this, in itself, will determine the style of rockery one can create.

Before determining the style, I will elucidate a little on the 'currant bun', for it is the one type of rockery, prevalent some years ago, that is no longer fashionable. A 'currant bun' is made from dough, indiscriminately dark or light in colour, hemi-spherical in shape, with currants sticking out in a haphazard fashion. It does not even resemble a rock cake. One will have seen many examples of the 'currant bun' rockery. A pile of soil scooped into a round mound with chunks of stone scattered liberally on the surface, not

One of the most famous currant bun rockeries in the world at the Physic Garden, Chelsea, London. In the background the architect, Hans Sloane – he of the square – surveys the rockery with a quizzical expression; and well he might, for rockeries were not invented when this statue was erected.

Good design

even stirred! This is the rock garden to be avoided. Possibly the most famous example of a 'currant bun' is the rock garden built in the Chelsea Physic Garden, London. It was built in 1772 and if it's good enough for Chelsea. . . It must be said that when this rock garden was created it was probably the first to be built in Britain and is still a fine example. As with everything fashion changes and more natural effects are expected today. The Physic garden is, however, well worth a visit.

Primarily, one must decide which style of rockery will be most in keeping with the general garden theme and the type of rock that will be most in keeping with the surroundings. The style of the rockery is determined, to a large extent, by the type and size of rock that can be used. Having determined access, one has determined the size of rock that it is feasible to transport. A rock the size of a flattish pillow is about 50 kg (1 cwt). A rock which looks good in a rockery is about twice this size.

There are two main styles: the first is to make the whole programme appear as natural as possible; the second is to replicate nature but to do so in miniature.

If one is commissioning a landscaper it is extremely important to predetermine the style of a rockery and, as far as possible, specify the type of rock. Sketch the finished effect three-dimensionally (or ask the landscaper to do so). Pace out the area in the plot. Is it too big/small/ overpowering? Eventually, one hopes, a compromise between reality and merely risible will be reached.

Not fashionable today

More research is required now, whether you are doing it yourself or commissioning professionals. Visit your local garden centre and study the rocks on offer. This allows an appreciation of the weight/size ratio, possible colours and rock types.

The next part of the research is for the more energetic, but is also the most fun. Take yourself and a camera for some long country walks, ensuring, of course, that the walk will take you near some rock falls, streams, etc. Take photographs of the effects you like and wish to recreate. Showing these photographs and indicating rock size preference to your landscaper will quickly clear up any early misunderstandings. It will also allow you to speak from a position of authority. Above all else the contractor will both appreciate and understand that you wish to be thoroughly involved in the entire project.

CHOOSING THE RIGHT SITE

The vast majority of alpine plants require sunny positions and south-facing is best. Few mountain peaks have the shade of a semi-detached suburban to overshadow the plant life and it is unrealistic to expect alpines to achieve healthy growth in, for them, unnatural surroundings. Try not to position the rockery under trees for the same reasons. Additionally trees will cause the soil to dry out and reduce the nutrients available. Finally, trees will drip water in winter which alpines most assuredly detest and the autumn fall will encourage pests and diseases if the leaves are left. This does not, of course, preclude a screen of trees if sited to the rear of the rockery as long as they do not cast shade. The reverse of this coin is to plant Ericae, many of which prefer semi-shade, and Ericae if not quite as colourful as alpines will provide year round colour.

A rockery looks better, or rather, more natural, if it is constructed on an incline. Again, an incline can be constructed but do try to get a machine of some kind to shift the earth. If access is not available it is easier by far to import topsoil and build up rather than excavate by hand and shift the resultant pile. If you are lucky enough to have a garden with an undulating surface then do consider the rockery as a method of creating split levels or an interesting rock outcrop.

BUYING THE PILE

As a general rule try to buy local rock. Much of the product cost is actually transportation and although 10 tonnes of rock may sound a lot it is only half a truck load to a quarrying company. Few companies are prepared to deliver less than a full load of 20 tonnes direct to a client, although the saving will be quite large. Before you contact a quarry, visualize 400 bags of cement in your back garden. For that is about the same cubic quantity. As a guide, 1 tonne of sandstone will yield about 30 pieces of rock which in turn will cover 4 sq m (5 sq yards) of flat rockery. If one wishes to create a cliff effect one must triple the quantity. In the main though, explain the concept to the garden centre and they will advise on the likely amount required. Be forewarned, however. As with most things in landscaping there are no industry standards: rock is bought by weight both metrically and imperial and by volume in cubic yards or metres. Some establishments merely price by eye whereas others will charge by inch, centimetre or gramme.

Always buy the largest pieces which can be handled through the access point. Nothing looks worse than 30 scattered 'bits' masquerading as a little mountain. Finally, remember for every tonne of rock one requires a tonne of topsoil. As I mentioned in the beginning, use the professionals. It really is not worth increasing your health insurance premiums!

TYPES OF ROCK

The most readily available products fall into two main categories, limestone and sandstone. If you wish to grow lime-hating dwarf rhododendron or heathers then choose a sandstone. Alpines will be healthier in a limestone. Limestones tend to be rugged, stratified and creamy white to dark grey in colour range, whilst sandstones are usually angular, non-stratified and usually coloured dark brown, often streaked with purple and green. Slate is good to use especially as part of a water feature and although granite or marble are acid and not particularly encouraging to plant life they do come in the most fantastic colour ranges from aquamarine to black via blue, pink and every imaginable combination. Plantsmen tend to avoid them; designers recommend them. At the end of the day the choice is yours. Unless one is a true 'avant gardener' who would use rock colours as an artist's palette, then basically one should attempt to either tone or contrast with the dominating colour feature in the garden, which, for most people, is the house.

It is possible to purchase man-made concrete rock which has the decided advantage of being lighter than the real thing. The examples I have seen are, however, uniformly uninteresting and expensive. Similarly, glass fibre products are on offer but currently (i.e. 1986) they bear little relation to the real thing.

BUILDING THE ROCKERY

As should be obvious by now this book is not about DIY and it is not my intention to explain in fine detail how to move rocks or actually build the rockery stone by stone. However, in order for you to persuade the landscape contractor to do the job properly here is what should happen.

OUTCROPS

When the site has been selected, as much as possible of the intended contouring should be carried out prior to receiving the first rock. Having created the anticipated layering, select the most interesting and possibly the largest rock, now called the keystone. This keystone is the guide-line for everything else and it will dictate the final outcome of the rockery. It should be placed about 30 to 40 per cent below the surface and firmly bedded in. If it is stratified then the strata should be horizontal; the remaining rocks should run parallel with it. Naturally, the keystone should appear as if it is part of a much larger rock that is running back into the soil and should be gently angled to accommodate this effect. Working outwards from the keystone, more rocks should be added with constant attention paid to matching both strata and colour. It is of vital importance that the stones look as though they should be in proximity to one another. Do not worry if the landscaper beds in a rock firmly and then decides he does not like the look of it and removes it altogether. Neither should you worry about telling him if it looks wrong – you will have to live with it for longer than

Left: Low rockery with rocks set close following strata lines.

Below: Japanese-style rock and scree. The rocks are positioned as an art form in their own right, without floral frippery. The differing-sized scree epitomizes wind ruffling the sea's surface.

he. In an outcrop, the rocks should not be too close together, but then one will have taken photographs of the real thing during the initial rockery research.

THE CLIFF
This is where most rockeries go wrong. This is where a pile of rocks looks like a pile of rocks. The paramount point is to ensure the rock faces complement each other in colour, size, shape and strata (see below). Again,

Fig. 21 *To create a more natural effect, check the direction of the strata lines which should then run approximately horizontal. Remember that in nature strata lines were created over the millenium by layers of material being subjected to enormous compression. Ensure all the weathered faces face out and that they incline backwards at approximately 15° to assist drainage.*

the keystone will determine the eventual shape and it must be selected with care. Angled slightly backwards the other rocks will be built up in layers on and around in much the same way as an outcrop, but steeper.

NEXT TO THE HOUSE
Building a rockery against a fence or against a building makes the purists squirm. Unnatural they cry. However, a rock outcrop in the middle of a town house garden is not particularly natural either. If a rockery will breathe interest into a wall with a barbecue set between it, then let it be done, as long as it is done well.

There are some basic precautions that must be taken care of, however. If the rockery is to be cited against a house wall, apply a coat of bitumen to the wall so that the damp-proof course will not be bridged. Then build a concrete block wall about 10 cm (4 in) from the house wall or fence to the required height and shape of the intended rockery. Ensure it is set on proper footings and apply another coat of the bitumen solution. Key it with sharp sand and set about the creation of the rockery as described earlier.

Left: Attractive example of a cliff face installed in high-rise garden in Wimbledon.

Below: In Mr and Mrs Conroy's Japanese-style garden in Barnes, London, three rockeries were created. This example has an Anglicized feel to it because of the proliferation of plants.

ADDING WATER

The problem with water on a 'natural' rockery is that it will run everywhere but the channel it is supposed to. Again it is a matter of selecting the right rocks for the job and positioning them correctly. If one is considering a waterfall that will run anywhere near the house then builder's polythene or plastic pool liners should be loosely draped under the intended water course, and the rocks and soil built up on top of the liner. Both the header pool and the water channel should be built up with mortar which includes a proprietary waterproofing agent and, just before the mortar sets, soil or peat should be rubbed in to colour the mortar.

COSMETIC FINISHES

Pea shingle or scree should be added to the finished rockery. It aids weed control and can soften and hide any nasty bits of mortar that should not be seen.

Finally, if my words have not deterred you from having a go yourself, then I wish you all success. Building a rockery, whilst hard work, is immensely satisfying. The final tip is to research thoroughly and sketch exactly what you expect the finished effect to be. Prepare yourself fully and above all, take your time. You'll need it.

8 · A CHILDREN'S GARDEN ·

A garden used by children, as opposed to one designed for children is usually quite easy to recognize. It normally looks as if wild animals have been let out.

There is the 'run': this used to be turf but for seven months of the year it is a triangular mud patch where wellington boots, bicycles, pedal cars and similar vehicles hit the edge of the patio at the run and spread across the lawn at 45 degrees. Then there are the scratch marks on the fence where it would appear the animals are trying to escape. This has in fact been caused by a combination of cricket/football/netball or any other ball game you may care to mention. Again, it is distinguished by the inevitable mud patch. In many gardens one can also find metal climbing frames and swings not dissimilar to those found in zoos which are provided to satisfy simian dreams of the African forest. Moreover, one can never forget the plastic pools that litter summer's landscape. In short, a garden used by children is not the sort of place to take tea on the lawn when Royalty drops by, but it can be very different.

The point about children is that they grow up, and fast. The metal swing that you install for the three-year-old will not take the weight of a child of twelve. The child of twelve is more interested in a trapeze or a track for the BMX bike. If you have, or are going to have children then you can plan a garden that can be either created at the very start or built up in stages to suit the child's age. More importantly, however, it should also be created to suit you.

THE CLIMBING FRAME

There are few garden features more attractive than vines or climbers spilling in profusion over a natural pergola. Treated timber will last for twenty years or more today and it will take several years for a pergola to be completely covered with plant growth. Using heavy timber approximately 10 cm (4 in) square, an attractive pergola can be created which will double as a climbing frame and swing for the first few years. A slide can also be incorporated for removal later.

Excavate 10 cm (4 in) of earth under the climbing frame and fill it with sand as a safety factor. The earth can be retained for use in a rockery. In the meantime, of course, the uprights for the entrance to the pergola will be just the right size for a goal mouth. As a further safety factor and particularly if the children are very young, ensure the climbing frame section of the pergola, if it does stretch the width of the house, is positioned to be seen from a room at the rear of the house.

PREVENTING THE MUD PATCH

Quite easy really: stop the children playing in the garden. This, of course, will prove not only impossible, but the very reason one buys a house with a garden is so that the children can play there. There are two practical courses of action that can be taken. One is to rotate the heavily used area around the garden in much the same way as cricket wickets are moved during the course of the season. The second method is, I feel, a little tacky, but it depends on how much bare earth offends you. Replace the well used turf with plastic grass or simply keep a roll of it to throw down when the children are playing ball games. There is a third option of course, and that is to reseed or returf the area each autumn. (Not during the soccer season!)

PREVENTING THE BMX SKID PAN

Toddlers or sub-teens, nearly all children will have a bicycle or other wheeled conveyance which will rip a bowling green to shreds. The best way to prevent this is to create a track for them to practise on. This naturally, will double as a winding path for you to perambulate, at a steadier pace, around your property. Depending on cashflow the path can be made from shingle, brushed concrete or slabs but if you use shingle ensure you have retaining boards at the sides and that a firm sub-base of crushed limestone scalpings or a dry mix of sand and cement is used. One can also utilize the dry stream concept and thus build a small wooden bridge over it to provide the 'wheelie' part of the course.

THE WATER FEATURE

As previously pointed out a water feature can bring a garden alive. However, a child can drown in even a few centimetres of water. One way to prevent this and still be able to plan a water feature into the garden is to create the pool and fill it with play sand. It can then double as a sand pit until the children are old enough to appreciate the dangers. An extension of this idea is to build a second pool at a different depth which can be filled occasionally in the summer months. The pools themselves should be

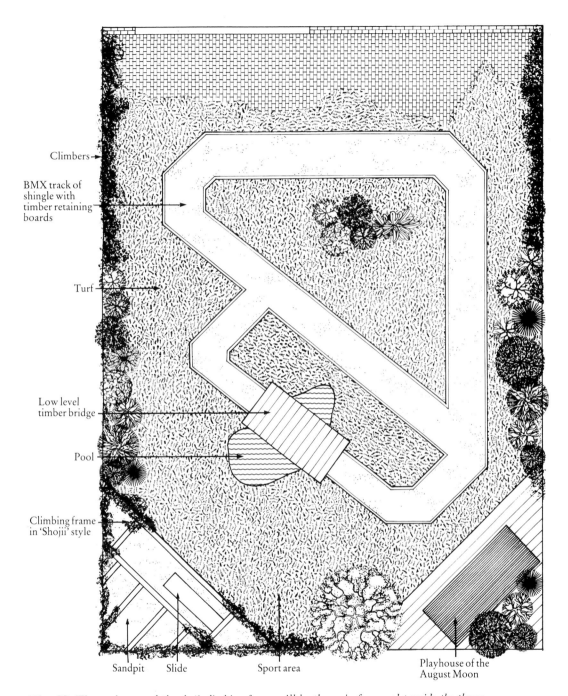

Climbers

BMX track of
shingle with
timber retaining
boards

Turf

Low level
timber bridge

Pool

Climbing frame
in 'Shojii' style

Sandpit   Slide   Sport area

Playhouse of the
August Moon

Fig. 22 *The tea house and the shoji climbing frame will be the main focus and provide the theme which the low bridge continues. The pool can be filled with sand for the first few years and, if they fall off, the offspring should not be damaged too much. The main patio can be brick or timber, but do include the path to avoid an otherwise inevitable mud patch.*

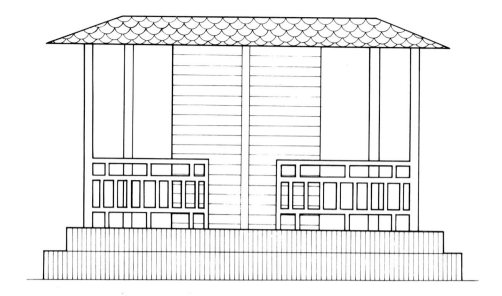

Fig. 23 *Common tool shed with false roof and timber frames to give a 'Tea house of the August Moon' effect. In this presentation it has been raised on a timber deck. The shed and verandah should be painted or stained to unify the whole.*

Bamboo

Weeping w[...]
cherry or sir[...]

Shed stained
red and black

planned to overflow into one another and the water recirculated by means of a pump. As you have had the foresight to plan all this and install the pump at the same time, you will be able to empty the pond after each bathing session by attaching an odd piece of hose pipe to the aforesaid pump and directing the water into a convenient flower bed.

THE PLAYHOUSE

Another important part of children's fantasy play is, for some inexplicable reason, to pretend they are grown-ups. To be a grown-up entails having somewhere to live and entertain one's friends. Hence the playhouse. The garden shed is the natural double for the playhouse but again one must be careful to ensure all dangerous chemicals and equipment are out of harm's way. If one wishes to be really adventurous then the front of the shed can be added to, to make it look more like a house than the ubiquitous creosoted variety. For the truly inspired the shed can be created as part of the theme for the overall garden.

Fig. 24 *Designed as a garden for children, the overall theme comes through strongly to be enjoyed by adults too.*

Shojii climbing frame
in red-stained timber

Trellising painted
red and fixed
to wall

CREATING A THEME YOU CAN LIVE WITH

We have identified five areas that children will utilize in their play: climbing, ball games, a bike/car/pram track, water/sand, and a fantasy playhouse. We need to draw these elements together and meld an overall effect that you will also be happy to live with (see Fig. 22). It is the shed which will really determine the theme. You can create a false front quite easily that might represent a miniature Georgian house, a castle or a thatched cottage. Then you simply design the rest of the garden within that theme. The example created here is mock Japanese.

The pergola is changed slightly with boards cut to shape and fixed on to the main frame to represent a *shojii* or 'heavenly gate', or even a goal post. The water feature is a rockery with a waterfall and two pools with the pump hidden in a submerged sump to prevent little fingers from damaging themselves. The water trickles through a cement water course set with pebbles and surrounded by silver sand. The inclusion of the pebbles ensures the water cannot collect in pools. It can easily be diverted to fill the second pool if and when one wishes. Leading on from the 'spring' is a dry stream over which a small bridge is placed with the path created from limestone chippings. The shed is readily available from garden centres and features a verandah to which a Japanese style pattern of lattice work has been added (see Fig. 23). Finally, add the mandatory bamboo behind which the boys can play Tarzan or soldiers and the girls can re-enact *Passage to India*. Who knows, you might want to join in too.

9 · DESIGNS FOR THE DISABLED ·

Gardening is now an accepted therapy for many people who have become permanently injured through car accidents, strokes or severe arthritis. The various garden activities exercise different parts of the body; fingers, arms, back and legs and even apparently simple tasks like hoeing or pricking out seedlings actually require major efforts of concentration and co-ordination. These activities, co-ordinated by and with the assistance of a trained therapist, can assist the rehabilitation of those among us who are unfortunate enough to suffer physical disabilities.

The other situation that has to be faced by us all is that while we live longer we will not necessarily be ambulatory for the rest of our lives. If you are living in the house of your dream and intend to stay there forever it might be worth adjusting your landscape in recognition of the inevitable.

Principally, a garden for the disabled or elderly needs to be simple: smooth flowing contours for paths (at 80, few people want ski ramps or the ability to do wheelies!), sufficient turning room for wheelchairs, hand rails and, above all, raised planters.

PATHS

To accept a wheelchair, a path would ideally be a minimum of 1 m ($3\frac{1}{4}$ ft) wide and provision should be made for a turning circle 1.2 m (4 ft). The surface should be as smooth as possible but remember it could become slippery after rain. Timber decking should have a milled surface to make it non-slip. Similarly, paving should have some kind of pattern or relief etched into the surface to allow for grip. Paviors or engineering bricks are ideal but do not use cobbles or small pavers as these may be prone to lifting in snow or ice. It goes without saying that the sub-base should be concrete and the slabs, paviors or bricks should be mortared down and pointed. However, if one wishes to use 'council' paving slabs or large slabs of Yorkstone then the weight of these products should allow them to be laid on sand without too much movement. One should avoid laying 'man-made' paving slabs on sand because they will inevitably shift and cause pot-holing or breakage.

Concrete is perfectly acceptable but remember it is going to be a broad swathe slicing through the garden so it should have a brushed surface and if

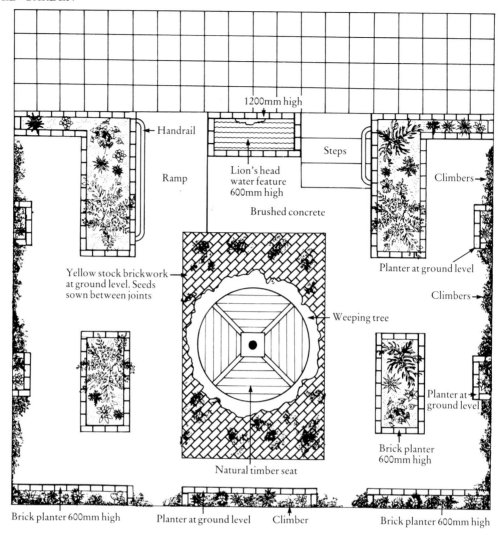

Fig. 25 *This design is based on a sloping site and has both a ramp and steps. The brushed concrete is suggested as a smoother alternative to paving and can look attractive if done correctly. The planters and the water feature are all planned at the same height to allow access from a wheelchair. Turf and trees will be needed to soften the harshness of the predominant hard landscaping.*

possible it should be dyed during the mixing process to co-ordinate the colour with other hard surfacing in the garden. Finally, if a wheelchair is going to be used one must, of course, replace any steps with a ramp.

BORDERS

Maintaining borders is a difficult and time-consuming task in the best of circumstances. If one is in any way disabled, the task takes on Herculean proportions. The simplest method is to reduce the width of the beds and replant with ground cover. Ground cover planting is ideal in that the plants reduce the maintenance requirement by taking up all the space where weeds might grow. Carefully selected for the soil conditions, they can also provide year-round colour. Additionally one could consider using one of the different types of forest bark to cover the bed. This not only looks attractive as a top dressing, but also helps considerably in reducing wind-blown weed seed.

RAISED PLANTERS

It would still be advisable to have raised beds constructed preferably with access to all four sides or alternatively some fairly large tubs where cut flowers for the house can be grown. For ease of working, a planter should not be more than 1.2 m (4 ft) wide and the optimum height for wheelchair working is 60 cm (2 ft). If access is not available all round then the width should be restricted to 60 cm (2 ft). The alternatives to a brick-built planter are fairly obvious: timber sleepers, split logs, short palings or almost any kind of timber. Remember that there will be a considerable weight of soil to support so ensure that any timber structure, with the exception of railway sleepers, should be at least 45 cm (18 in) into the ground and if a support post it should be encased in concrete. Timber should be tanalized or similarly treated and to prevent further rot from damp soil run a sheet of builder's polythene between the soil and the timber itself.

If a person is severely handicapped, it may not be possible for them to work from a sideways position. If this is the case your clever landscaper should be able to design a purpose-built planter similar to a low desk, in that a chair can be placed giving the person the ability to face the planter with their knees underneath the 'work surface'. The planter can be made from fibre glass or glass-reinforced concrete and should be stepped to allow different depths of soil. Naturally it must have drainage with a fine mesh over the drain hole and preferably an accessible 'U' bend to stop too much soil erosion. A cheaper method would be to indent the planters with 90 cm (3 ft) spaces and place an old fashioned 'Belfast' scullery china sink over the opening. The difficulty with this latter method is depth of soil but by selecting alpines and similar plants that do not require deep rooting this difficulty can be overcome. At this point most designers will waffle on about hypertufa. (This is a mixture of sand, peat and Unibond builder's adhesive which is caked on the side of the sink to make it look like stone; it actually looks like gunk.) If one must disguise a perfectly elegant piece of utilitarian design then why not just paint it; in pastel shades or primary colours if it co-ordinates well?

Climbers

Ramp

Brick planters

Yellow stock brickwork at ground level

Brushed concrete

Fig. 26 *This garden assumes that a person's disability will confine him to a wheelchair. Although illustrated here on a slope it will also translate to a horizontal site.*

HANDRAILS

In the chapters covering Victoriana and water gardens mention has been made of using timber balusters and handrails for both balconies and bridges. There is no reason why this attractive effect cannot also be used for assisting the disabled in the garden. Where there is a ramp or steps, install a handrail. It is preferable, of course, to use hardwoods in an exterior situation, but hardwoods too should be treated with either varnish or paint. Budget permitting therefore, use hardwoods but as treatment has to be applied one could use softwoods as long as care is taken on regular maintenance. The handrail, naturally, should be as smooth as possible and fixed at a convenient height which is normally 90 cm (3 ft). If using timber ensure the ground rail is bolted into a concrete block or similar at regular intervals to ensure rigidity.

There are several alternatives to timber, such as concrete balustrading or wrought iron. Concrete balustrading should only be used if your garden has a Georgian theme; moreover, one would need a fairly large garden to take the dimensions of this type of product. Due to its size it also has the disadvantage of being difficult to grip, but the other side of the coin is that one can sit on it to take a breather.

Wrought iron can be used in any situation where a timber balustrade is feasible. It is, however, a specialist job to install. One last inexpensive item is a steel gas or water pipe. With so many people refurbishing old houses these old pipes are readily available from junkyards, even skips. You need to be quite tough to undo the existing joints and you will probably have to hire pipe bending and cutting equipment and specialist tools to cut new threads where new joints are to be inserted. The steel will last for ages and with a coat of co-ordinating paint the finished effect could look very attractive. As well as placing handrails in the obvious places such as steps and slopes as previously mentioned consideration should also be given to their emplacement around areas of maintenance. For example, a climbing rose will need deadheading, a dwarf fruit tree will need harvesting. Logic will determine the best places for installation.

MINIMAL PHYSICAL MAINTENANCE

Readers will have noticed by now that I prefer technology to traditional skills. In a garden for a disabled or elderly person technology comes into its own. The purists may whinge but it seems ridiculous to me for someone to struggle weekly with the lawn mower when a chemical spray can retard grass growth to an extent where the weekly trauma is reduced to twice a year. The grass is cut in the spring, sprayed and cut once more in the autumn. These retardants are similar to the products used for slowing the growth of hedges but as the average gardener makes his money from maintenance he is unlikely to tell you about it; if pressed he will explain that chemicals are bad for the garden. Which is the same point made by the medical profession about the introduction of penicillin.

Fortunately there are landscape gardening companies who will carry out chemical maintenance on a garden on a twice yearly basis. The process is basically one of determining the major problem areas and then spraying weedkillers, growth inhibitors and nutrients in spring and autumn after which very little weeding or other maintenance is required. Farmers have been using similar products for years and unless one is a total masochist it is silly not to take advantage of the available help. This maintenance programme is much less expensive than the jobbing gardener, and if the jobbing gardener was a window cleaner last week what, seriously, can you expect?

Under this heading comes another boon for the handicapped gardener, automatic watering systems. These are available as a DIY installation and consist of a micro-chip sensor, an automatic valve, an optional pump, and either flexible or rigid piping and spray heads. The valve is attached to the mains water system and the valve is activated on a time switch via the sensor which determines the amount of water required. If it has rained the previous evening the sensor will not switch the water on. If the ground is parched then it will operate the switch until the required amount of water is distributed. The piping is plastic which facilitates easy jointing and is laid 45 cm (18 in) below the surface. The spray heads are fixed by means of a T-joint and are usually placed 15 cm (6 in) above the surface. For a lawn, pop-up spray heads are available or an alternative is to use piping laid in parallel lines with drill holes every 8 cm (3 in). These pipes are laid 8 cm (3 in) below surface and the water simply weeps out. This latter lawn system is obviously best installed when a new lawn is being laid. Automatic watering is not expensive and not only is it labour-saving but it can be timed to switch on early in the morning rather than last thing at night. If one were a plant, one would prefer it this way! It means less evaporation and sufficient moisture to last the day. The other advantage, of course, is that the garden will be watered when the gardener is away on holiday. Which is usually at the hottest time of the year.

TOOLS

There is a huge range of tools available for the disabled or elderly, and frankly a lot of them can be used by fit gardeners as well.

A telephone call or visit to your local garden centre is one way to determine the best tools for the job but additional information, and in some cases demonstrations, can be found by contacting the various Institutions listed at the end of this chapter. In the meantime I have refrained from listing the tools generally available for, apart from reading like a manufacturer's brochure, individual disabilities require certain specific products. It is best to try them out for yourself.

FURTHER INFORMATION

The Disabled Living Foundation,
346 Kensington High Street,
London W14 8NS

The Gardens for Disabled Trust,
Headcorn Manor,
Headcorn,
Kent TN27 9NP

The Royal Horticultural Society,
Vincent Square,
London SW1 2PE

10 · CO-ORDINATED COLOUR SCHEMES ·

In today's world of instant everything the garden is virtually the only area left untouched. Many will argue that this is as it should be; the garden is for all things natural, and as such it should take time to mature. I for one am not convinced. For many years now nurserymen have been forcing a wide variety of plants and, if you can afford it, mature shrubs and trees are always available. Moreover, although a newly landscaped site is usually a dramatic improvement on the original, one inevitably hears the phrase 'Just wait until it has matured'. Regrettably this situation is unlikely to change because of the vested interests in the gardening industry. In the meantime, you the consumer are the final arbiter. Unless and until more demand is made for a higher standard of design, quality and convenience in domestic landscaping products then nothing will change. In an attempt to correct this situation in a small way, I have been experimenting with timber effects recently, operating on the premise that a garden could reflect the internal decor of a home. By using prepared timber and paint, one can ignore the inherent constraint of natural materials and progress to much wider concepts of design. Furthermore, as one has the flexibility of colour application, a relatively 'finished' effect can be created in a few hours.

COURTYARD COUTURE

An example of this design philosophy is this unusual courtyard created for lovely Patricia Wood at her London home in Chiswick. She is a marvellous client who understood intuitively the effect I was trying to achieve. The garden is overlooked from the dining room and, as eating or entertaining is not a completely passive situation, the visual effect can be somewhat 'active'. The courtyard was walled on all sides and was fortunately south-facing. Originally the garden sloped upwards away from the patio doors, which in due course might have created drainage problems. A small lawn had been laid, which, in common with similar sized courtyards, created more trouble than it was worth. Yet another common problem existed in that the garden was surrounded by houses on all sides but previous to my arrival, the judicious use of trees and climbers as screens had done a lot to alleviate the problem.

I decided to link the garden with the dining room itself and create an

Colour co-ordinates. Blue of dining-room transmutes exterior to become a garden room.

Fig. 27 *Pool shape complements patio quadrant and screen guides the eye from dining-room vantage point in this exciting modernist design. Strictly a garden for the stylish.*

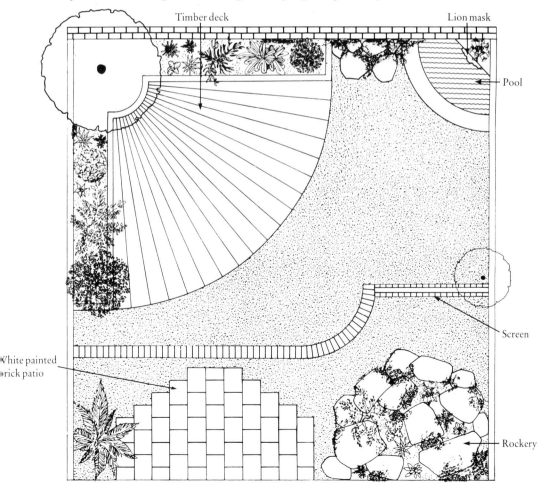

Timber deck

Lion mask

Pool

Screen

White painted brick patio

Rockery

'outdoor room' effect by extending the cool blue colour scheme to all raised horizontal surfaces. A patio was required for pre-dinner aperitifs, and an interesting focal point that could be viewed after dark. The solution for this tiny area was finally that of a raised patio constructed from timber quadrants painted blue to co-ordinate with the dining room and a small raised pool with a lion head mask providing a continuous waterfall. The screen was made from timber and, when viewed from the dining room gives extra depth to the courtyard and leads the eye over the foreground rockery through to the water feature (see Fig. 27). Spacing between the vertical wooden spars of the screen is critical as it should not restrict visual access to any part of the garden, unless, of course, there is a particularly unsightly vista that one wishes to obscure. Having carried the blue colour scheme into the garden I decided to use white as a complementary colour. Granite chippings make up the scree which, although slightly off white, add a variable texture to the horizontal surfaces and also blend well with the rockery.

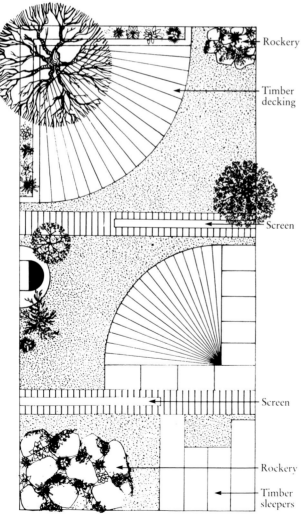

Rockery

Timber decking

Screen

Screen

Rockery

Timber sleepers

Fig. 28 *Extending the theme of the screen to guide the eye, this layout allows a second, almost secret garden, where alternative activities can take place.*

Above: Screen directs vision of observer to water feature, creates second garden and is additionally a 'stand alone' feature.

Left: Inexpensive lighting creates an even more dramatic environment and doubles the time the garden can be enjoyed.

Most of the structural planting was well established and care had to be taken during construction not to disturb the roots, but as Patricia had decided to be her own plantswoman the photographs shown were taken before she completed her planting. The garden was finished with some inexpensive but effective lighting. This type of garden may well be too structured for the traditionalist gardener but I feel quite strongly that it is the shape of things to come. It allows co-ordinated colour schemes, and not only provides colour year round, but also gives you the ability to ring the changes very simply. Maintenance, of course, is minimal.

HARRY'S BAR

In Britain the wine bar phenomenon is still a growth industry where individuals, as opposed to the major brewing chains, can still make their mark in establishments which are both highly original and atmospheric. The secret of success lies in the personality of their owners whom, as a breed, are normally strong entrepreneurial characters with a shrewd eye for developing trends. The owners of Harry's Bar are no exception and not only did they realize the interest in *al fresco* eating created by holidays

Colour scheme follows corporate colours even to the selection of hanging baskets. Raised deck lifts previously drab concrete courtyard.

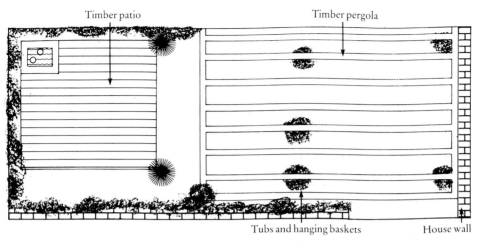

Fig. 29 *Corporate colour scheme extended into garden area. Just think what could be done for IBM!*

abroad but they also recognized that a large expanse of potential selling area was being under-utilized in the concrete backyard. When I was approached to design and construct a courtyard garden, speed, naturally, was of the essence. The interior design is strongly modernist with a dramatic red and black colour scheme. An answer to the dual requirements for an 'instant' garden in keeping with the company colours was found by using wood to provide a raised timber decking and a pergola effect which unified the whole area into an outdoor room. Strategic spotlighting was added to enable evening usage and a barbecue and additional bar were built into an existing external garage. A water feature was installed in the shape of a

For a bar the choice of statue was virtually mandatory.

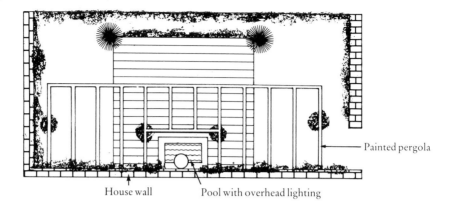

Fig. 30 *For the smaller garden, pool is introduced into patio with pergola.*

square pool with a statue providing a continuously recycled fountain. The statue may seem a little obvious retrospectively but the patrons were generally amused by the joke. The concrete floor was painted with black concrete paint and the trestle tables and walls were painted white to 'enlarge' the area. Hanging baskets and tubs completed the ensemble and it should be noted that the plants were also selected to colour co-ordinate. To speed up the construction programme the timber was cut to size and the priming and undercoats were applied with a spray gun as were the walls and tables. Two coats of topcoat were applied, the first using the spray gun after carefully masking the area with newspaper whilst the final red topcoat was applied with a conventional brush. It took two men a mere five days to completely transform a large, dirty and dreary storage yard into a bright and friendly bar and barbecue area. Consider the possibilities for your own external entertainment area.

THE AUTHOR IN PINK AND GREY

My wife Gabrielle and I are the sort of people who move house when it either needs redecorating or we become bored with it. We enjoy the challenge of redesigning and remodelling both the interior and exterior of a new property to such an extent that we have moved six times in the past seven years. After a time one loses track but one tiny garden that we both enjoyed is illustrated here and the new owners, Nigel and Veronica Bowland, kindly allowed us back to photograph it. At this time we were coming to the end of our pink and grey period although as I write it is still a very popular colour scheme. We chose these colours as an extension of our dining room which just overlooks the garden. The property itself was a small, late Victorian, artisan's cottage and built when gardens were

The author in pink and grey.

considered too much of a luxury for the working classes to enjoy. The backyard, therefore, was big enough to contain a copper and a mangle to facilitate Monday's washing and very little else.

When we moved in the backyard had been concreted over and left bare. As the overall dimensions were 5.5 × 4 m (18 × 13 ft) it would initially appear that there was not much more that could be done. The normal solution that is applied to these situations is to lay slabs or brickwork and grow a few climbers from tubs. Fortunately for us the neighbouring gardens had been established for some time and all the foliage you can see in the photograph had come from these adjoining plots and thus we merely had to 'decorate' around it.

One other major disadvantage was that the house was mid-terrace. If we had considered laying turf (and I assure you we did not) the concrete would have had to be excavated and carried through the house and similarly if we had paved the area then more sand, cement and bricks or slabs would have had to come in the opposite direction. Always one to plan around difficulties, the timber decking became an obvious alternative (see over).

Our basic requirement was for somewhere to sit and entertain which meant a decking area of 2.5 sq m (3 sq yd). The rainwater drainage from the house was a surface gully that ran over the concrete base; we had the alternative of excavating a new sub-surface drainage system or raising the deck. The benefits of installing new drainage were far outweighed by the

Painted timber patio

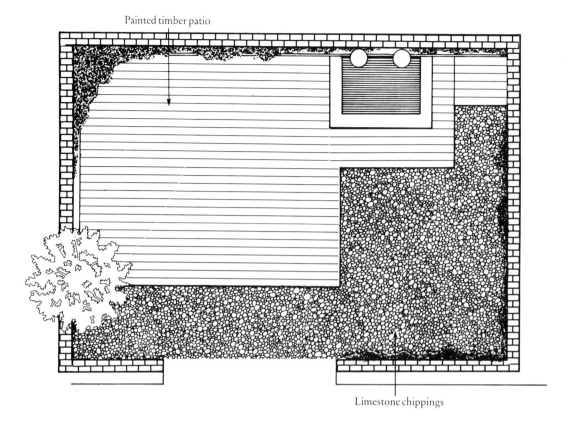

Limestone chippings

Hedera etc growing from
neighbour's garden!

Pink painted trellis

Lighting

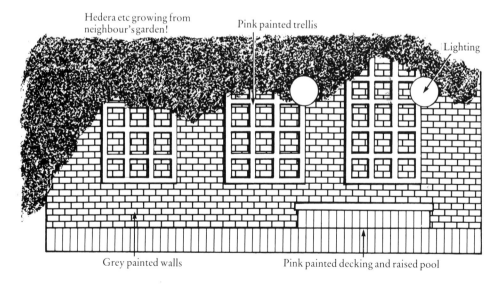

Grey painted walls

Pink painted decking and raised pool

Fig. 31 *Cover concrete with limestone scree and spray walls a matching shade of grey. Paint remainder pink. Profile shows raised pool, pink trellis and lighting. Presto! The art of avant gardening.*

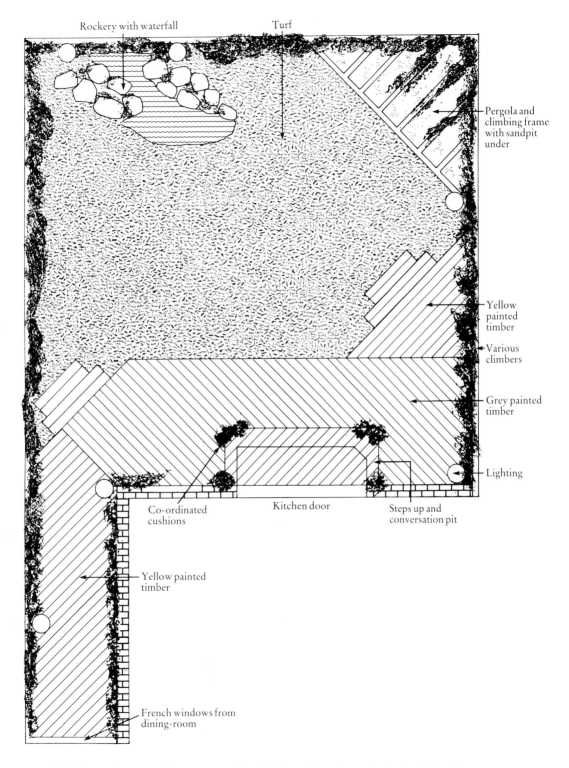

Rockery with waterfall

Turf

Pergola and climbing frame with sandpit under

Yellow painted timber

Various climbers

Grey painted timber

Lighting

Co-ordinated cushions

Kitchen door

Steps up and conversation pit

Yellow painted timber

French windows from dining-room

Fig. 32 *This is the proposal for my current London home where the garden is viewed from the kitchen, predominantly white and the dining room, a combination of pastel yellow and grey.*

cost and, in any case, a raised deck solved the problem and had the dual advantage of being more interesting. I have always been keen on water features but with two small children at their most inquisitive stage alternative provision had to be made. The pool was built with a pond liner and can easily be drained and filled with sand. In the meantime by raising the sides it prevented the children from walking straight into it. When filled with sand the reverse is true in that they can climb out easily.

Having overcome the inherent difficulties by deciding on the easiest and most simple solutions out came the trusty spray gun. All the vertical surfaces were sprayed grey and the horizontal surfaces pink. The trellising was bought as standard 1.8 × 1.8 m (6 × 6 ft) panels and cut to size then painted, and the local timber yard cut the decking to size before delivery. All in all the garden took one person two days to paint and fit. This, truly, is a fitted garden.

11 · PITFALLS, PRICES AND PLANNING ·

I first created the Fitted Garden philosophy in 1979 and the word has been spreading ever since. My good friend Richard Bartlett came to work for me as Construction Director in 1984 and understood implicitly what I was attempting to achieve. When I decided to concentrate on writing and design he started his own landscape construction company and understands the pitfalls and problems better than most. The following chapter is largely based on Richard's experiences and should be studied well, particularly if you are commissioning landscapers to create a garden for you.

EMPLOYING THE PROFESSIONALS

The Fitted Garden concept is an extremely novel one; perhaps this is why it often seems to provoke fits of uncontrollable hysteria among the more traditional elements of the landscape industry. However, during these bouts of 'constructive criticism' one of the most basic essentials of garden design is being totally overlooked. People discuss the principle of garden design evolving naturally and complementary to its owner and surroundings; basically they mean that the garden in question should 'fit': fitted *au naturel* to its surroundings, fitted to perfection to the client's tastes and, moreover, fitted expressly to the client's budget. The only gardens I know of that have evolved naturally are probably deemed 'wild' and these are usually the very gardens one is presented with for revamping.

Apart from my conviction that gardens should fit, I believe that a client and their chosen landscaper should also 'fit'. Hopefully in this chapter I can offer some advice on how to achieve this – 'a garden without tears'.

The basic structure of the landscape industry is very simple. With large schemes and commercial projects one's main involvement will be on a fee basis with landscape architects and constructionally with landscape contractors. With general domestic schemes one's involvement will be with landscape designers and landscape gardeners. The remaining sections of the profession briefly comprise gardeners (general soft landscaping and maintenance work), tree surgeons (specialists) and horticulturists (specialists in soft landscaping). Most, if not all of these sections of the industry will hold professional qualifications and therefore have all the necessary skills, back-up, insurances, etc.

However *caveat emptor* – let the purchaser beware! One unfortunate by-product of our industry, as with the building industry, is the amount of 'cowboy' firms in existence. 'Anyone can plant plants, lay paving slabs and turf; well, it comes in rolls like lino!' are commonly heard phrases and they represent a frightening précis of a very complicated profession. Green fingers are one thing but green gardens like good wine mature with age as a direct result of the level of professional attention at their conception.

Most local newspapers and area Yellow Pages carry advertisements for Landscape Garden Design and Construction services. Some will be large combines, e.g. Garden Centres and Nurseries while others will be two or three man bands. Some, one finds are affiliated to certain institutions, e.g. BALI (British Association of Landscape Industries) or the Guild of Master Craftsmen. Admirable though these institutions may be they are not a guarantee of professional expertise in either design or workmanship.

Interview at least three or four companies prior to commissioning any work in a garden. Instigate a brief 'chat' period indoors prior to setting foot in the garden concerned. However brief this initial encounter, I believe it is an essential phase prior to the actual commissioning of the project. It gives one the opportunity to sound out the landscaper himself and gives him the opportunity to absorb the interior of your domain together with your own persona. This is so very important if you are both to 'fit'. Although this may seem obvious, try it on yourself even if your option is a DIY garden. Examine your own home, your personal preferences and talk to your partner and the family. The resulting experience and expectations may even surprise the most self-assured. Divorce is one sure way of acquiring a garden of one's own choice.

BUDGET

Although your landscaper will consider a garden as an 'outside room', most people do not imagine it in this context; surprising, really, when one considers many families spend thousands on their kitchen and bathroom and then stand or usually fall back aghast when it is suggested that a budget of £2000 is required to enhance their 'tiny plot outside the back door'. Budget, as in all things, is one of the most important factors governing the potential success or failure of any project. Having spent £6000 on refitting a kitchen of say 4×3 m, although it may be as up-to-date and automatic a kitchen as 1986 permits, it is still a room in which one would like to avoid spending time. Hence the recent vast increase in quantities of dishwashers and au pairs. To expect to acquire a utopian garden setting of, say, 20×5 m ($65 \times 16\frac{1}{2}$ ft) for £750 still leaves most landscapers speechless, if only for a few seconds – one has to earn a living after all. Furthermore most people will pay handsomely to have a kitchen or bathroom fitted by 'professionals'.

A garden differs only in as much as the individual creativity will cost less than the trappings of inside but the 'fitters' are true professionals. Remember a landscaper has to be 'all things': a gardener (planting and turfing), a builder (patios, paths, walls and ponds), an electrician (lighting), a plumber (ponds and water features) and a sculptor (rockeries).

Do investigate finance, i.e. HP and especially extending an existing mortgage, as some Building Societies are also 'Garden Societies', the more so as gardens are now acceptable as home improvements and may qualify for tax relief.

DESIGNS AND PLANS

Always request a plan of the potential garden drawn to scale. A garden designer will charge a fee for the design. One must therefore be comfortable with the various styles and creative output before they are commissioned. As with landscape architects they will also charge a supervisory fee. On the other hand the more talented landscape gardeners will include the plan in the price of the garden. The problem here is that one is not comparing like for like. One plan may be more complex and therefore more expensive. If the intention is to commission landscape gardeners direct then draw a very simple plan of your own and ask them all to quote against it. This will define the cost parameters, if not the quality of work. Having determined the price level, set a budget and request they design to it. Apart from indicating the level of the potential landscaper's professional expertise, this will ensure not only that both parties are aware of exactly what the finished project should attain but also enables each quotation to be compared like for like. Should any alterations arise during the project either by your own request or due to unforeseen ground conditions or the like, a plan provides a benchmark for recording these alterations.

The plan should also be used to assist in one's understanding of the project prior to signing any contract. Pace out the areas of the garden yourself. Ascertain whether the intended patio is going to be too large or too small, whether the planter walls are the correct height and check that the pond is going to be a major feature or a large 'puddle'.

This is no reflection on the potential landscaper. Plans are by nature sometimes difficult for the layman to understand most especially from the aspect of visual interpretation. The most vivid and traumatic example of the need for plans is when commissioning a rockery. Photographs of existing rockeries are wonderful when viewed in the comfort of one's armchair but one should remember that these are pictures of mature, established creations usually in isolation from the actual garden they reside in. Before the planting becomes established these wonderfully corruscated gems appeared as 'bland' as your initial rockery will seem, no matter how imaginative the landscaper may be. To avoid one of the worst landscape follies, the 'currant bun' rockery, convey your ideas, demand 3D sketches and investigate the suggestions offered in depth. No landscaper worth his salt will be upset over a seemingly pedantic display of concern with any aspects of the design. In point of fact, as he appreciates, a well thought-out rockery can be one of the most delightful aspects of a garden. I have paid for earlier disasters; proper planning will ensure your salvation.

SPECIFICATIONS AND SCHEDULES

A professional company will provide detailed specifications of the work entailed on the project. This should cover both materials to be used and sequence of work operations. Obviously this will complement the plan and enable one to understand the quantities and types of materials the potential landscaper intends to use. This is an invaluable document when it comes to comparing the various quotations and has the added bonus as a vehicle for determining the costs of any alterations that may prove necessary during the contract. Again, with kitchens or bathrooms one can obtain brochures showing the assembled products in detail. With a garden this is almost impossible. Always request samples of the materials to be used or visit the local garden centre and view the products first hand. Brochures are notoriously unreliable when considering colours and textures. One valuable tip is that having obtained a sample of, say, paving, soak it in water. This will give a clear indication of the intended patio's appearance in winter when the weather is predominantly wet and overcast. Reputable landscapers will select rockery stone personally but do visit a local supplier to satisfy yourself on colour and texture as it can prove rather difficult to bring four or five samples of rocks weighing 200 kg each to your home for your perusal. Finally, schedules will define all the different operations to be performed, the sequence of these events and the expected duration of the project. Compare the schedules and their accompanying quotations to assess value for money. Patio slabs laid on sand will appear cheaper than on a sub-base of concrete or hardcore. Quality, however, remains quality.

PLANTING SCHEDULES

Having decided on the overall garden design, request a schedule identifying the various types and position of the intended planting scheme. The landscaper will need to work this out in consultation with you and it is not therefore an unreasonable request. Ensure you have specified likes and dislikes in colour, texture and size. Planting schedules are also invaluable to maintain an aftercare programme for a garden and most gardeners will be happy to offer a maintainance contract.

SAMPLES OF WORK

Initially ask for photographs of the potential landscaper's previous contracts or visit the gardens in question with him. Better still do both. If he is truly bona fide his previous clients will be only too pleased to show their garden to you.

QUOTATIONS AND CONTRACTS

Avoid all mention of estimates, request quotations! Read quotations carefully! Are they inclusive or exclusive of VAT? Are they fixed price or fluctuating depending on the intended start date? Insist on a properly signed contract for both parties and make sure all parties sign and incorporate the plan and specification into the contract. Should any alteration arise during the course of the project, it is essential to obtain the costs in writing *before* sanctioning the work. Amend the plan and specification accordingly with the date and alteration clearly stated.

GUARANTEES

Although it should be general practice throughout the industry to offer guarantees on work, sadly it is not so. A bona fide operation will have no hesitation in doing so; few will guarantee plants as so much depends on aftercare, but for paving, walling, ponds, etc., insist on at least 12 months.

PAYMENTS

Compare the methods of payment. On projects of say 3 to 4 weeks duration there may be a request for stage payments. This is not uncommon and for the smaller companies is a fair request. Despite the opinion of some, the landscape industry is not that lucrative. Cash flow, like the weather, is a constant problem.

FINALLY . . .

A garden is the most individually creative improvement to any home and one should become thoroughly immersed in all the differing aspects. A kitchen can be easily changed, a room redecorated. A garden not so; a garden achieves its ultimate glory in maturity. A garden is one area where one can realize the true extension of spirit; whether through a professional landscaper or self-created one must both live with it and in it for a very long time.

DOING IT YOURSELF

Naturally I must declare my bias towards employing professionals as that is how I earn a living. However, if one has in mind a Duke of Edinburgh Award for bravery by all means go for it. Arm yourself with a few hundred gardening books and at least two garden sheds worth of tools, brew a large pot of coffee and wait for the rain to stop.

The increase in local garden centres and DIY outlets has made it easier (not a lot) for the layman to attempt his own garden project.

So what are the pitfalls here?

PLANNING

Although it is fun to roam around one's garden and discover the various features do remember the overall layout should be an extension of your interior and as such be generally viewable from within. Spend time sketching out various different layouts and then decide on an overall theme.

Buy a compass! Establish how the sun affects the different areas of your garden, plan your patio and lounging areas to suit (sunbathing in a shrub bed is uncomfortable). Mark out areas roughly first with pegs and string lines, this will give you some idea of scale and the amount of preparation involved. With complex shapes try using sand to mark the parameters; sand lines are very easy to adjust to your initial changing ideas.

When planning planting areas, read your planting books *carefully* to establish exactly the different growth rates and final size. Structure your beds accordingly. Try to produce all-year-round colour as there exists a lovely variety of trees and shrubs which will brighten up the most miserable winter's day. Plan for minimum maintenance, shrubs and groundcover plants will mean less weeding.

If you do get too 'bogged down' with ideas most landscapers will offer a design-only service. The fees are very reasonable but do remember these plans will have a copyright – use them carefully.

SITE PREPARATION

This is the secret of successful gardening. Do not skimp on preparation whether it be wall or patio foundations or preparing ground for turf and planting.

Most garden centres sell soil-testing kits – *buy one*. Use it before you plan your planting scheme.

This is where the hard work is; do not take short cuts, do engage the services of a good osteopath and start saving up for a jaccuzi!

If during initial excavations (yes, you are going to have to *dig*) one encounters an underground air-raid shelter from bygone days (it will always be exactly where you want your patio), then I recommend you move house. Do not in any circumstances contact a landscaper (The Society for the Prevention of Cruelty to Landscape Gardeners has a long arm.)

PATIOS

Slabs, blocks, bricks or timber, the choice and variety is staggering. Just ensure your foundations are adequate. Patios are for lounging on, not a newly acquired hobby in garden maintenance. Be careful with your design: curves are attractive, but complicated cutting especially on slabs is time-consuming and expensive. Take care with levels and drainage. Do consider timber patios which, apart from the variety of finishes one can achieve, they are much easier and less backbreaking to construct.

WALLS

Plan your shapes and heights carefully. Subtle curves are all very well on plans but can reduce even the most Rambo-like bricklayer to tears.

Foundations again are most important, even if the walls are only to be dwarf planters.

If this is to be your first attempt at bricklaying may I suggest that June 21 (the longest day of the year) is the time to start. There is something quite rewarding in lounging on your new patio with a large gin and tonic admiring your own prowess as a bricklayer. Equally well I know of more people that swallow vast quantities of gin (no tonic) as a result of this initial baptism!

My most sincere and heartfelt advice here is to assume an air of totally suicidal depression and patronize your local pub's endless supply of bricklayers.

ROCKERIES AND ROCK GARDENS

The frustration of building a rockery to match your initial concept is the surest way I know to 'find religion' (you will also discover why the Japanese use so few rocks in their designs). 'A thing of beauty but an eyesore for ever' I hear people mutter prior to committing *hara-kiri*.

There are no real secrets to success, I'm afraid. Just make sure the core is soundly constructed and is self-draining and arrange your rocks as your imagination dictates. Do try to ensure, however, that you have a clear picture of your basic requirements and experiment during construction.

Be patient (although with most rockeries in small gardens consisting of one or two tonnes of material it is a somewhat difficult creation to rush anyway).

Be bold with your planting; do not restrict yourself to just heathers etc. Go for a variety of shapes and sizes to give more structure.

Renew your earlier acquaintance with your osteopath.

WATER FEATURES

Water is wonderful: it will give even the most beautiful of gardens an added air of tranquillity for a very small outlay. As well as fountains, ponds, waterfalls and streams why not consider a dry stream as an alternative?

Virtually everything you will require is readily available from your local garden centre. Do read the instructions carefully and you will then discover one of the most enjoyable of all garden creations (I expect you did not realize this when you were fighting to maintain your sanity while building that rockery – a pity as a waterfall can be a wonderful feature in a rockery).

LIGHTING

Easy to install (at last I hear you cry), but did you remember to lay the cables under your patio before you laid those 10 tonnes of slabs?

Lighting can transform the most interesting of gardens into a wonderland overnight (or more to the point at night). The most dramatic displays can be achieved by the subtle placing of lights.

Whether this be in planted areas or in ponds and waterfalls the secret is to hide the source from the eye. From any vantage point in the garden one should only be able to see the illuminated effect of the object not the lamp itself.

I would recommend you contact a landscaper who specializes in garden lighting for although the installation is relatively simple, planning the position and layout of a scheme calls for a particular talent to achieve the ultimate effect.

PLANT (MACHINERY), TOOLS, ETC.

Various mechanical aids are available nowadays including excavators small enough to pass through doorways. There are excellent varieties of power tools available, especially important when cutting slabs are guillotines and the small electrically driven portable cement mixers are a must. This equipment is best obtained from your local tool hire shop, the hire rates are very reasonable and a lot cheaper than the cost of a specially designed orthopaedic truss.

Wheelbarrows (plural) are mandatory primarily to transport the 20 tonnes of material you will eventually have somehow managed to lose in your garden. Surprised? – that is why as I mentioned earlier £750 for a complete garden leaves me speechless.

Do not skimp on tools. Get the best and a sensible selection. A healthy body is more important than saving a few pounds.

12 · MATERIALS AND FUTURE TRENDS ·

I view the actual setting of the garden as more important than the flora. Whilst plant selection is important it is after all the finishing touch. A rectangular lawn with rectangular borders may well have beautiful flowers and shrubs, but how much nicer they would look in a garden that has been specifically created to receive them.

One of my main criticisms of the landscape industry (and I am by no means alone in this) is that, relatively speaking, there have been no new construction products introduced for 2000 years. A designer can have superb creative inspiration, but having to use traditional products means actual construction is labour-intensive and slow. Take, for example, brickwork. A skilled bricklayer can lay 1000 bricks a day, if it is in a straight line and no one is going to examine it too closely. However, a brick built edifice in a garden has no other value than being attractive. Therefore, when you lay back on your lounger sipping gin and tonic you will actually examine the workmanship. The pointing must be perfect, the joints all to an exact size and profile. Under these conditions it is unlikely that the most skilled of landscapers will lay more than 400 bricks a day, hence the relatively high cost of landscape construction. There are some building systems around today that will allow the keen DIY type to produce a certain standard reasonably fast. These systems are largely based on buying moulds which are fixed *in situ* and concrete poured into them. They are demoulded 24 hours later and hey presto, one has a garden wall – of sorts.

One of the reasons why I like to use timber in the garden is that a variety of effects can be achieved inexpensively and fast. Many will say timber rots in our climate and I would agree. However, manufacturers now produce a wide range of external paints and treatments that help protect timber from the vagaries of climate for periods up to 20 years. As with everything else fashions in garden design change a great deal in 20 years. The modern consumer will change their internal decor every four or five years. Why not the external decor too?

In the meantime one is currently restricted to traditional materials and time-consuming and traditional skills but the following are, in my opinion, the best of the bunch.

Modular hard landscaping with Blanc de Bierge setts, steps and slabs.

BLANC DE BIERGES

J. Delvaux is a Belgian company that created an award-winning modular system-building technique specifically for landscaping. The actual product is basically a brushed concrete sett that comes in one colour, creamy white, but has nearly 500 different but complementary components. In addition to the previously mentioned setts there are slabs, reversible steps, spiral staircases, kerbs, wall copings, planters, seats and swimming pool linings.

More modules from J. Delvaux's Blanc de Bierge.

Construction is based on traditional sand and cement but if one is looking for co-ordinated concrete this is the product range to specify. As the photographs depict, some superb effects can be achieved.

RECONSTITUTED STONE

Many companies manufacture reconstituted slabs and bricks which are much much cheaper than the original natural product. Much like the brickmaking industry the largest companies dominate the market to such an extent it is a virtual cartel. In a way this has helped to raise the manufacturing standards of the products on offer but it has also had the effect of reducing consumer choice. If you have a monopoly why bother to introduce new products? In almost all areas of the country, however, there are small companies producing their own slabs. They cannot get distribution in garden centres and/or DIY superstores because of the cartel but manufacture primarily for their own use as landscapers. Some of the slabs they produce are very unrealistic so demand to see a sample and keep the sample to compare against the product that is delivered. Also ensure that the product they use is properly cured for both the small companies and the large are notorious for delivering 'green', i.e. uncured slabs.

The point to be made is that if you select one of the small local producers, and watch them like a hawk, you will probably get your patio supplied and laid for the same price as buying the materials from one of the majors. That said the best and most innovative of the major products is probably Bradstone, manufactured by E. H. Bradley in Swindon, Wiltshire.

Marshall's Old York paving creates path. Note path laid just below lawn level so that grass can be mown right up to the edge without risking the mower blades.

Reconstituted stone slabs: Marshall's Mono Saxon Paving with coarse-textured surface finish.

Naturally they are also slightly more expensive but nonetheless their reconstituted products are the most realistic of the mass manufactured brands and are readily available. English China Clays' 'Countryside Masonry' is on a par with Eternits' Atlas Stone Company in both product and price whilst the cheaper and more utilitarian slabs are produced by A.R.C. under the 'Broadway' brand and Marshalls under their Marshalite brands. All these manufacturers produce bricks or walling blocks to match their paving slabs. Once you have studied the market place, however, you will probably join me in wondering where all the innovation is.

PAVIORS AND PAVERS

To this day no one has successfully explained to me the difference between paviors and pavers. Suffice to say they are similar to slightly undersized bricks, come in two thicknesses dependent on the application, and used in the right circumstances can look superb. Many people have had good results with ordinary house bricks when laying paths or patios but it should be discouraged as ordinary bricks absorb a great deal of moisture and will split or flake once penetrated by frost. Paviors are made specifically for these conditions and come in an enormous range of colours. The other major advantage of paviors is that the larger size, normally $215 \times 102.5 \times 65$ mm thick, can be laid on a 8 cm (3 in) sand bed, butt-jointed and bedded down with a vibrating plate. (This latter can be rented from any hire shop but one must ensure a rubber, rather than steel, plate is fitted.) This method of laying either patios, paths or driveways has much to recommend it. The products themselves are manufactured to British Standards and once the site has been properly prepared the actual laying can be extremely fast. One still has the normal materials-handling problems

Blockley's paviors laid on sand facilitates faster construction.

however. The smaller size of pavior, nominally 215 × 102.5 × 50 mm or 33 mm thick are also available in a wide range of colours and textures. This size, although cheaper, must usually be laid on a mortar bed with mortar joints thus requiring considerably more skill and time. It may, of course, mean that less subsoil has to be excavated in the first place but if you are considering having paviors laid as part of your landscaping scheme have a quotation for both types prepared. Ibstock, Blockleys and Butterley have good ranges.

POURED IN SITU

One method of 'paving' that is both fast and economic when there is a reasonable amount of hard surface work to be done is the Bomanite system. In essence coloured concrete is poured into prepared bays and a pattern is pressed into it with steel moulds. This is definitely not DIY as the system is a franchise operation (from America, where else?) but it is an economic alternative to traditional methods. Many landscapers, faced as usual with a too tight budget, often use an older but similar method. Again concrete is poured into prepared bays but the surface is brushed with a stiff broom to give an attractive surface decoration. Before you commission anyone to do this ask to see photographs of similar work!

GLASS, GLASS FIBRE AND PLASTIC

When I first started writing this book I had intended to include a section on more modern labour-saving techniques using materials more fitting for the latter part of the twentieth century. However, as yet they exist only in prototype form but if any reader wishes to have a truly avant garden please contact the Publisher and I will be more than happy to oblige.

NATURAL MATERIALS

If one is designing a traditional garden it would be bliss to specify natural materials but these days it is usually only the very rich, the State or international corporations that can afford them. For the privilieged few, and those architects working for non-rate-capped councils, here is a brief list of natural hard landscaping products.

SLATE
Slate is still quarried extensively throughout the United Kingdom and is

available in a range of colours from silver grey through all shades of green and blue to purple and black. Whether split, sawn or polished it is a most handsome and adaptable material that weathers and mellows beautifully.

YORKSTONE
Again a material that matures wonderfully and looks better after two centuries than it does after two years.

GRANITE
At one time granite setts were to be seen in most major cities and very attractive they were too. Today supplies are limited to second-hand stock and most people will have to be satisfied with the man-made equivalent.

MARBLE
Not a good product to lay as paving but it is seen in the odd shopping mall. In the Middle East some of the richer sheikhs have the joints between their marble paving slabs filled with gold, which, I suppose, puts it all in context.

HARDWOODS, SOFTWOODS
If it was not for the technical breakthroughs by the timber treatment people one would have to specify normally expensive imported hardwoods for exterior use. As Chapter 10 demonstrates, softwoods can now be used externally and wood is very effective in all its forms.

CHIPPINGS, SHINGLES
Ordinary washed shingle can be very effective and very cheap. Specify the size carefully for both the job you are doing and the effect you wish to create. Used sparingly, marble chippings are also moderately priced and can be purchased in a wide range of colours. Similarly the ubiquitous (for me) limestone chippings are also very useful.

THE FUTURE

Few people are aware of how large the market is for landscape gardening. One of the primary reasons is that the business itself is fragmented and there are no national or even large regional landscaping companies that specialize in domestic landscaping. Indeed, as many readers will have learnt to their cost, a large proportion of the unemployed become either window cleaners or gardeners in the belief that anyone who can handle a shovel can recreate Babylon's hanging gardens.

On a similar level few designers have progressed much beyond rehashing the Victorian rusticana of William Morris, and, if the general public are offered little other choice how will the industry change? It will change, I believe, for two reasons. Public demand and commercial awareness.

Today we enjoy more leisure time than ever before and a great deal of this time is taken up with home improvements. Even those who swear they would not recognize one end of a screwdriver from the other will happily plant a few flowers in their plot. This, you see, is not DIY or home improvements but creative gardening. Meanwhile gardening skills are extolled in books, magazines and newspapers, on radio and television but try as the amateur might it is extremely difficult to create a garden with the kind of cosmetic finish that one finds at the Chelsea Flower Show. In your home you probably have a fitted bathroom, bedroom and kitchen all of which can be installed with a modicum of intelligence and a little bit of toil. The finished result is usually very professional and the reason for it is simple. All the various parts have been mass produced to a very high standard, and, because the accoutrements and surrounding decor are your individual choice the final result is unique. Before very long the public will demand something similar in the garden.

The mass manufacturers of existing hard landscaping materials have a vested interest in not producing easy to use materials. Like a lot of British companies their R&D budgets are low and they are resistant to change and innovation. Moreover, the majority of their sales are to the construction industry who still use methods more akin to wattle and daub than the late twentieth century.

This attitude permeates the landscaping industry, both in design and construction. Why rock the boat when the customer has not (yet) complained? It is a vexed question over which I have had long discussions with many people in the business. The consensus appears to be as follows. Firstly, most designers enter the landscaping profession specifically because they enjoy nature, and quite rightly so. Similarly most of the actual landscapers join the industry for the same reason. Apart from earning a living, and few do more than scrape by, they have little motivation to explore new ideas. The result, if one analyses the rapidity of change in interior design over the past two decades in comparison with exterior design, is that one might be forgiven for thinking that landscape design and construction has remained in some sort of time warp.

Landscaping gardens in the United Kingdom alone is a business worth £600 million per year. That is more than the fitted kitchen and fitted bathroom business put together. Big business will eventually realize this and the changes will provide major advantages to the consumer. The first changes will be in the materials offered. It is inconceivable that when man is preparing to walk on Mars that we are still using materials that have remained basically unchanged since the Pharaohs: baked mud bricks. The new materials will be one fifth the weight of existing concrete products and will have the facility to resemble natural stone or wood more closely in both colour and texture. As well as duplicating natural materials these new products will be offered in co-ordinated colourways and in a range of differing textures. The most important breakthrough, however, is the inherent lack of weight. Basically it means one person will be able to pick up and carry a square metre of fully finished 'wall', position it in the garden and then 'glue' the next section to it. No concrete needed! Patios, paths and pools will be laid the same way, and think how easy it will be to construct a rockery.

When the existing design constraints of having to use unwieldy and expensive materials are released, landscape architects will be able to experiment with new and original ideas, much as their architectural colleagues have been able to do with buildings. It is also to be hoped that some of the more innovative designers from other professions will also be attracted to the exciting possibilities of exterior design. With the ability to predetermine the finished outcome of a garden in terms of design, quality, colour and effect, the way becomes clear for mass production techniques similar to those used in the fitted furniture business. In other words, by the 1990s you should be able to choose and purchase a Fitted Garden in the same way that you can buy a fitted kitchen, but in a wider choice of design parameters than are available to the gardener today.

Other new technologies are making their mark felt in landscaping. Watering the garden is not a particularly onerous task but is surprising how inefficiently it is done. One can count as legion the times that having laid a new lawn the owner will then proceed to turn the entire area into a sea of mud on the pretext of 'a good watering'. Come the water meters things must change! There are currently available several computer controlled watering systems that utilize an exterior sensor to test either precipitation or moisture levels and then automatically switch on the water to the required amount. A complete system can be supplied and fitted into the average garden for less than £250 and, come the water meters, will no doubt pay for themselves very quickly.

Several of the larger nurseries now control their plant stock on computer and will also provide you with a planting programme if you ask. They feed data on soil type, climate, aspect and your favourite colours into the data base and presto, pick up your plants at the payment desk. Once this system has been allied to computer graphics you will be able to design your garden, pick out your colour scheme and create your garden in a couple of weeks. If you think this is particularly futuristic then see your kitchen showroom. They have been using the system for years.

If any reader is worried that all the spontaneous creativity could be lost to gardening may I reassure them at once. Anyone who does not wish to have an individually planned, easily built, maintenance-free garden brimming with blooms need not. Gardeners have done it the hard way for centuries.

A final note to make the traditionalists' hair curl. I understand it will soon be possible to create life-size holograms in the open air. A hologram, as you are no doubt aware, is a three-dimensional photographic image that looks dramatically real. Instead of planting plants one will dial the image required and have it reproduced electronically. Until one tires and decides on something new. At which point publishers will publish lists of top ten garden holograms.

The future then is one of great promise: better materials, some of which could be preconfigured to make hard landscaping much easier and cheaper to carry out; designs and planting programmes on computer which will allow almost anyone to plan a successful garden at very low cost; inexpensive computer monitoring of essential garden maintenance and low level tasks; and, if all this is still too much work, dial a number and change your view. Daily.

Interested readers, and manufacturers, are invited to write in if they would like tomorrow's technology today.

Index

Arbours, 20
Atlas products, 119

Balustrading, 93
Bar garden, 100–2
Barbeques, 34, 101
Blanc de Bierges, 109
Blockleys, 41, 121
Blocks, pitch-faced, 58
Borders, for disabled, 90–91
Bradstone, 118
Bricks, 107
    edging for pool, 68
    planters, 26–27, 34
    terrace, 50
Bridge, timber, 42, 65
    wrought-iron, 63–65
Broadway, 119
Budgeting for landscaping, 119
Butterley, 121

Chemical retardants, 93–94
Children's garden, 83–88
Chippings see Granite; Limestone;
    Marble
Cliff-type rockeries, 80
Climbing frames, 83
Colour coordination, 10, 96–106
Computer system for landscaping,
    124
Concrete, balustrading, 93
    brushed, 117
    flooring, 102
    paths, 89–90
    poured in situ, 113
    rocks, 78
Contracts, 111
Countryside Masonry, 111
Courtyards, 23–24, 96–100

Damp-proof courses, 34, 80
Designing, 109
Disabled, garden for, 89–95
Drainage, 103
Dry landscape garden, 38
    streams, 50–52

Eternits, 111

Fountains, 18

Glass, 121
Glass fibre, 121
    rocks, 78
Granite, 114
    chippings, 98
    rocks, 78
Guarantees, 122

Handrails, 93
Hanging baskets, 68, 102
Hardwood see Timber
Herb beds, 20
Holograms, 125
Hypertufa, 91

Ibstock, 121

Japanese gardens, 35–47

Keystone in rockery, 35–47
Knot gardens, 22

Lake, 63–65
Landscape garden industry, 114–7
Landscape gardener, employing,
    107–8
Lawn, as play area, 84
    chemical spraying, 93–94
    semi-circular, 52
Leaf-fall problems, 25–27, 62
Lighting, 101, 124
Limestone chippings, 41, 122
    -hating shrubs, planting, 42–43
    rocks, 78

Marble, 114
    rocks, 78
Marshalite, 119
Maze, dwarf, 22
Mechanical tools, 114

Orchards, 21
Oriental gardens, 35–47
Outcrops of rocks, 78–80

Parapets, 21

Paths, curving, 14–16
    for bicycling, 84
    for disabled, 89–90
    shingle, 58–60
    Tudor-style, 21
Patios, 123
    raised, 33, 55–60, 98
    tiles, 16–17
    two-level, 68
Pavers, 112
Paving for disabled, 89
    riven slab, 33–34, 58
Paviors, 112
    Blockley, 41
    brick, 27–29
Payment methods, 122
Pea shingle for rockeries, 82
Peat beds, 43, 47
Pebbles as pavior infilling, 29
Pergola, 83–84, 88, 101
Planning the garden, 109, 122
Planters, brick, 26–27, 34
    raised, 91
Planting schedules, 110
Plastic, 121
Playhouse, 87
Pools, brick-edged, 68
    cleaning, 62
    for children, 84–85, 88, 106
    liners, 65–66
    raised, 98
    siting, 61–62
    square, 102
Privy garden, 18–19

Quotations, 111

Railings, for disabled, 93
    Tudor, 19
    Victorian, 14
Ramps, 90
Random pattern garden, 47
Retardants, chemical, 94
Rockeries, 27, 58, 71
    building, 78–82, 124
    planning, 73–76
    siting, 76–77
Rocks, buying, 77
    in dry stream bed, 52

sizes, 75, 76
types, 77, 78

Samples of landscaper's work, 121
Sandpits, 62, 84
Sandstone rocks, 78
Schedules, 121
Scree in rockeries, 82
Screens, timber, 42, 68, 98
Sculpture, 102
    stone, 72
    timber, 23
Secret gardens, 18–19, 43–47
Shed, as playhouse, 87–88
    disguising, 68
Shingle, 114
    stream, 52
    path, 58–60
    surfaces, 50
Site preparation, 123
Slates, 78, 113–4
Softwood *see* Timber
Specifications, 110

Split level garden, 48–60
Spotlighting, 101
Squared garden, 21
Steps, paved, 60
Stone, *kotah*, 34
    reconstituted, 109–11
Stream, dry shingle, 50–52
Stumps of trees, 67, 71–72

Tea ceremony, Japanese, 35–38
Terraces, 50
Timber, 114
    bridge, 42, 65
    coloured, 96
    decking, 101, 103
    paths, 89
    railings, 93
    screen, 42, 68, 98
    sculpture, 23
Tools, 114
    for disabled, 94–95
Topiary, 22
Topsoil leaching, 60

Trees, leaf-fall problems, 25–27, 62
    near rockeries, 77
    stumps, 67, 71–72
Trellising, timber, 72
Tudor garden, 17–22

Victorian-style garden, 14–17

Walkways, covered, 21
Walls, 16, 123
Water gardens, 61–72
Waterfalls, 48–49, 62–63, 98
    in rockeries, 82
Watering systems, automatic, 94, 124
Willow, dwarf weeping, 52
Wood-retained path, 58–60
Wrought-iron bridge, 63–65
    handrails, 93

Yorkstone, 114

Zen-inspired gardens, 38–40